Foreword by Salima Rockwell

PUSH
THROUGH

Your Ultimate Success Playbook

HAWLEY WOODS & CAREY YUKICH

PUSH THROUGH

Your Ultimate Success Playbook
AUTHORS: HAWLEY WOODS & CAREY YUKICH

THE ULTIMATE PUBLISHING HOUSE (UPH) HEADQUARTERS

Canadian Office: 205 Glen Shields Avenue, Toronto, Ontario, Canada L4K 1T3
Telephone: 647-883-1758
www.ultimatepublishinghouse.com
E-mail: info@ultimatepublishinghouse.com
www.pushthroughbook.com
www.thepushthroughmovement.com

US OFFICE: Ordering Information

Quantity Sales: Companies, organizations, institutions, and industry publications. Quantity discounts are available on bulk purchases of this book for reselling, educational purposes, subscription incentives, gifts, sponsorship, or fundraising. Unique books or book excerpts can also be fashioned to suit special needs such as private labeling with your logo on the cover and a message from or a message printed on the second page of the book. For more information, please contact our Special Sales Department at Ultimate Publishing House. Orders for college textbook or course adoption use.

Please contact Ultimate Publishing House Tel: 647-883-1758

PUSH THROUGH HAWLEY WOODS & CAREY YUKICH
ISBN: 978-1-7354831-3-9

DEDICATIONS

Hawley Woods

In dedication of my two unborn children, may their souls rest gently in the arms of my Savior. Godspeed, babies...Mommy loves you. Furthermore, this book goes out to all the little girls who were told "No, not you, you're not good, smart or strong enough." May you use this book to Push Through and permit yourself to believe that YES! YOU ARE ENOUGH, YOU CAN, and YOU WILL!

Carey Yukich

This is dedicated to my mommy in heaven who always encouraged me to "kick it in!" May these words resonate with her spirit and empower the voice of many who, for whatever reason, don't speak up for themselves, but unconditionally shout to the rooftops for others. I say to you "Push Through!"

TABLE OF CONTENTS

ACKNOWLEDGEMENTS

Carey Yukich

Throughout my life many people have supported me and walked with me along my journey. I am grateful to all for their contributions.

My family:

My husband John Yukich, thank you for all you do to be my best teammate ever! You are my ROCK, holding my hand and being my biggest fan. Your unconditional love for me and our girls has provided a solid footing for me to "go for it." Our Heavenly Father knew what he was doing bringing us together.

My daughters Jess and Sam, know that you are braver, more beautiful, and stronger than you think. I love you and am proud of the young women you are becoming. My prayers for you both are that you will see in yourself all that God has blessed you with in your lives. Your father and I are in your corner, even as we challenge you to learn, work hard, follow your dreams, and push through any roadblock.

My mommy in heaven Lynn Nostrant, your unconditional love and incredible support still inspire me. Your huge heart, INCREDIBLE hugs, and courage have pushed me to take this leap. Your spirit comes through in many of these words, and your voice is heard LOUD AND CLEAR here. You are the definition of humility. I love and miss you every day! The best in me came from you!

My brother James Nostrant and sister Katie Nostrant, I am honored by our connection. James, thank you for helping with our mother. May you realize your potential and use these strategies to push through any obstacle. Katie, you have an amazing spirit and heart, just like Mom. Believe in yourself as you build the life you dream of, using your experiences as a guide. I pray you realize how you inspire so many with your smile and the light in your eyes.

My dad Jim Nostrant, your support and belief in me means more than you know. I love you.

My grandparents, Jim and Ann Nostrant, and Ray and Juanita McDonough, how blessed I was to have so much of you in me, and to have been involved in your lives.

My uncle and godfather Tom McDonough, thank you for all your love and support.

My sister/friends: Luba Balacky, Shawn Baldwin, Tonia Wallner, Crystal Hoffman, Stacey Kammes Wanshek, Renee Underwood, Joyce Richardson, Shelly Evers and Karen Artim.

My TrueWealth team: Jennifer Vinovich, Andrea Sullivan, Kyle Schmidt, Danielle Helfrich, Beth McCarty, and Michael Gordon. Thank you for your support, for all you do for our community and those we serve, your input, and incredible example of teamwork!

Our TrueWealth clients, thank you for trusting us and for being living proof of the Push Through concepts!

My coaches, who saw more in me than I saw in myself. You helped provide an example for the coach I became, and impacted many to push through:

- Chris Wernette of Morley-Stanwood HS girls' basketball.

- Beth Launiere of B.R.A.V.O (my volleyball club) and now University of Utah Head Women's Volleyball coach.
- Jerry Angle, thank you for making my college dream a reality and providing my scholarship.
- Rick Cedarburg, Ryan Moratti, and Lou Cassara for becoming my professional coaches.
- Pam Blalock and Rebecca Dunne, thank you for the example of women in leadership.

For all the interviewees for validating our Push Through concepts and willingness to share your wisdom

My sports teams: teammates at Cut Bank Junior High and HS, Morley-Stanwood HS, B.R.A.V.O, and Northwestern University.

The Altitude and Epic United teams I coached and those who I worked with through the recruiting process.

Hawley Woods, THANK YOU for walking through this journey with me, for teaching me so much about guts, and trusting enough in me to PUSH THROUGH.

H a w l e y   W o o d s

In Luke 12:48 …" From everyone who has been given much, much will be demanded;" Many people through the years have reminded me of this, and I thank you!

I thank my mom and dad for giving me life. I dedicate this book to them. May they RIP, knowing that their legacy lives on through me and my siblings.

Thomas Woods and Debi Orness, I thank you both for being an example of love, loyalty, and strength. The three of us can handle anything life throws our way. We laugh, cry, and love together. I love you both and would do anything in my power to make you and my nieces/nephews (Amanda, Tanner, Jade, Thomas, Nathanial) happy. You all bring me joy!

I thank my extended family, Erica, Ryan, Ginny Johnson, and Peter Jensen, my in-laws Bob and Cheryl Gray, as well as my Aunt Diane and Uncle Lonnie Woods for always loving and supporting me as their own. Through your example, I learned how to love a child as if he were my own. You are a beautiful reminder that family does not have to be blood. I love you!

Thank you to my Church of Christ family. You keep me grounded in the Cross and remind me that the Holy Spirit lives inside of me. Your prayers and love lift me up. Thank you for seeing and knowing my faults and loving me anyway.

To my Appreciation Family, thank you for teaching me how to help a lot of people, create life-changing wealth and improve every day. I appreciate the opportunity to serve and lead alongside all of you, especially the Moores, Team Synergy, and my team, The Way Makers.

Thank you to the WOW Women of Wealth ladies, Krista and Lisa. Those five years together are cherished memories. I love what you each bring to my life. All the ladies of WIFS and eWomen Network, thank you for challenging me and surrounding me with your strength and leadership.

To my teammates and best friends, Lori Courtney, April Devine, Kristin Ulrich, and my secret society of volleyball; Katie, Kathy, Beth, Deanna, Sherri, Janey, and many more, you are my sisters. I am forever grateful for your love, support, and friendship

Coach Kimball, Coach Poole, and Coach Compton, thank you for believing in me and giving me your wisdom on and off the court. Those hours of instruction have been used wisely–well mostly.

Thank you to my past bosses, Judy M., Doug P., Richard H., Lynn and Terry L. You gave me a chance to shine and taught me the valuable tools I use in my business today. Thank you to all of those involved in my PSI Seminars journey. I appreciate all my mastermind ladies, Nanette, Sher, Unison, Rachelle. I cherish our relationships, your love, and support.

Thank you to all the people who contributed to our book. You all have had an impact in my life in some shape or form. Thank you to the Ultimate

Publishing House and our fearless project manager Felicia Pizzonia. You and your team have done a great job bringing Push Through to fruition.

Carey Yukich, THANK YOU for taking this journey with me and saying yes! Your strength and commitment have provided me great insight to leadership. Your grit and work ethic give me the inspiration to continue to PUSH THROUGH!

Finally, I acknowledge my family. Adrian Rodriguez, you made me a parent and I love you. You have an opportunity to create an amazing life. There will be challenges, but you will push through with your love for God and your strength. I am proud of you and I'm always in your corner. Jackson Gray, my baby boy, you are my inspiration! You are smart, kind, independent, tenacious, and most of all loving. You are a true leader, my son. I look forward to supporting you in creating an incredible life. Finally, my life would not be complete without Bobby Gray, undoubtedly the single most important person to me. Thank you for sitting down every time I say I have an idea, saying I DO, and giving me this life and wonderful adventure. I admire the man of God that you are and how you lead our family spiritually. Faith, Family, and Freedom, you are my rock and you support me in the most selfless way. You are my hero and I love you deeply and completely. The best is yet to come!

FOREWORD BY
SALIMA ROCKWELL

The events that happen in our lives constantly shape us and force us to evolve. In my life, I've been fortunate to have had some amazing experiences, many of which revolved around one of the things I am most passionate about: the sport of volleyball. During this time, I have been thrown many curveballs but it has been through those very experiences that I have been able to conquer the challenges that I've faced. What Carey and Hawley bring to light in their book, *Push Through*, are the numerous principles that are taught, learned, and applied through playing a team sport. You will learn about yourself and what you can contribute to create a strong team, as well as how a good team not only helps you realize your best self, but also your role within it. Whether this team is your friends, family, or coworkers, it deserves the best YOU to be a part of it.

It's funny how something as simple as a game could have such a significant and indelible impact on my life. My greatest time of growth began when I entered my freshman year at Penn State University. My volleyball career, while seemingly easy from an outside perspective, was in fact a time of constant struggles and challenges. Through fierce competition, and a grueling practice setting that demanded nothing less than your best effort, I learned how to overcome nearly impossible situations. I grew to welcome and even embrace the challenges that were laid out before me. It soon became clear that having the ability to work your way through a tough scenario and come out victorious is one of the most rewarding and useful skills that one can acquire. I am fortunate to have had coaches and teammates who helped me build those skills as a foundation of my life. At the time, I appreciated them for how they helped me contribute to the team, but little did I know that these prolific experiences would also guide me through so many future opportunities. From Pharmaceutical Sales, to coaching and recruiting, I've realized that I wouldn't have excelled in any of those areas without the conscious and unconscious strategies I gained along the way. They would even guide me during one of the toughest times of my life—the aftermath of a major stroke I suffered in 2009. I was the mother of a toddler and newborn, facing a risky and terrifying situation. Along with support from my family and friends, I was forced to rely heavily on the tenacity and determination I gained in those formative years to restore myself to a better state. On the days that I wanted to give up, I would have loved to have a book like *Push Through* there to remind me that I had the qualities to successfully navigate my new way of life.

Push Through is a book of action that not only provides you with a roadmap to success, but also a playbook for you to take real and measurable steps to achieve your goals. Through stories that reveal intense emotions and impactful moments, Hawley and Carey take you into the hearts and minds of true champions of life. You will learn what drives them from within to help you arrive at the place where aspirations turn into achievements. The authentic way they have shared their insights and success playbook will warm your soul and ignite a fire in your belly to strive to be better in every aspect of your life.

Today, I have transitioned into a television broadcasting career, and while my experience has brought me to this point, the strategies offered in this book are what have contributed to my continued success and growth. At a time when life can seem unmanageable and the world is full of chaos, a book like *Push Through* is a refreshing and welcomed resource that everyone will find incredibly useful. I am thrilled to support Carey and Hawley on their journey in helping others find their own ways to "Push Through" life's challenges and uncover the best version of themselves.

Salima Rockwell

PAVING THE WAY

1972 was a big year for both of us, despite being toddlers. Congress passed Title IX, officially known as Title IX of the Educational Amendments of 1972. Since that day it has grown and been refined and is now a catalyst for athletic achievements for women across the United States.

At the heart of the amendment is this statement: "No person in the United States shall, on the basis of sex, be excluded from participation in, be denied the benefits of, or be subjected to discrimination under any education program or activity receiving federal financial assistance." Sports were meant for all who desired to have the opportunity to participate and any school receiving federal financial assistance was obliged to create the same opportunities for women provided to men. What a game changer for female athletes!

When Title IX was first passed, we were both too young to realize what it would mean in our lives one day. However, as we grew into our athleticism and started to have life goals, the amendment and what it stood for took on a powerful meaning and changed how we chose to pursue our future interests. Its existence allotted us the opportunity to compete in the sports we enjoyed at the collegiate level and further our education, which helped us develop the traits that would make us successful athletically, personally, and professionally.

The hard work, grit, character, integrity, and efforts of many people before us gave us this chance. However, Title IX was only the beginning. It would take far more fine-tuning to the system to level the playing field. One of the biggest obstacles to conquer was that many athletic departments were not funded through federal assistance. It took nearly fifteen years for this blind spot to be remedied so women could have more opportunities. It was an uphill battle full of hard work, lobbying, and rallying for the outcome we received, but after fighting for a fair share for the female population, it finally happened.

The dedication of every person, both women and men, to fight for equal opportunity to participate in sports led to Congress further defining Title IX. Today, this groundbreaking piece of legislation serves as the hand of fairness and equality in the world of athletics, giving countless opportunities that women only a few decades ago never could have dreamed of. We are thankful to:

- Congresspeople and advocates for women's athletics who fought to make sure the vision contained within Title IX came to fruition
- Those individuals who supported the opportunity
- Schools working to create the programs that would allow female athletes to participate

Thanks to these people's efforts, by the time we were starting college in the late 80s, we entered it knowing our academic options were far more open with the expansion of athletic scholarships for women. We knew exactly how lucky we were to be able to take advantage of this opportunity, so squandering it was not an option. We were determined to work hard to make sure we gave ourselves the best futures possible.

Sports changed us, mind, body, and soul, to become stronger and more confident. It gave us the tools we needed to lead better lives and succeed in ways that wouldn't have happened without them. Whether in our daily lives, careers, or in a match, we picked up some of our best traits from being athletes, teammates, and coaches. However, our lives would look quite different were it not for the brave men and women who fought for our equality. We offer a heartfelt "thank you" to all those who gave us the opportunities that changed not only our lives, but the lives of female athletes now and for generations to come. You have given countless women a foothold where few previously existed. We will always strive to do you justice.

TIMELINE OF TITLE IX'S DEVELOPMENT

Here are the key dates for advancements in Title IX that have helped it to achieve its goal and objective for fairness in sports.

June 23, 1972: Title IX of the Education Amendments Act enacted by Congress and signed into law by President Richard Nixon. It prohibits sex discrimination in any educational program or institution receiving federal aid.

September 1973: Three years after permitting women, the University of Virginia fields women's basketball, tennis, and field hockey teams.

May 20, 1974: Sen. John Tower of Texas proposes the Tower Amendment, which would exempt revenue-producing from determinations of Title IX compliance. The amendment is rejected.

September 1974: Old Dominion becomes first college in Virginia to offer athletic scholarships for women.

May 27, 1975: President Gerald Ford signs Title IX athletics regulations and submits them for Congressional review.

February 17, 1976: NCAA challenges legality of Title IX.

August. 1976: Virginia Tech makes steps toward women's athletic program. Women's basketball (previously a club sport) and swimming played their first varsity seasons in 1976-77. Volleyball, field hockey began varsity seasons in fall 1977.

September 1977: University of Virginia, William and Mary offer first athletic scholarships to women.

December 11, 1979: Department of Health, Education and Welfare issues policy interpretation on Title IX and intercollegiate athletics. Implementation of the so-called "three-prong test" is required for compliance.

1980: Department of Education is established and given oversight of Title IX compliance through the Office of Civil Rights.

February 28, 1984: Supreme Court limits scope of Title IX in case of Grove City College v. Bell. Court rules that Title IX applies only in areas that receive direct federal funds, which removes athletics from the equation.

March 22, 1988: Civil Rights Restoration Act of 1987 enacted into law. This Act reverses Grove City decision and restores Title IX to institution-wide coverage, including athletics.

August 1988: Hawley Woods enrolls in United States International University in San Diego, CA.

August 1989: Carey Yukich enrolls at Northwestern University in Evanston, IL.

August 1991: Hawley Woods transfers to Arkansas State University in Jonesboro, AR.

GAME ON!

"Excellence is about fighting and pursuing something diligently, with a strict and determined approach to doing it right. It's okay if there are flaws in the process – it makes it more interesting."

CHARLIE TROTTER

Meaningful growth is easy to want and hard to achieve. Really, where do you even begin? For us, sports brought out tenacity, courage, perseverance: truly the best versions of what we were always meant to be. Our athletic careers gave us a small-scale view of how life worked. We saw the world in x's and o's and that gave us a playbook for success. Whether you are a lover of sports or not, meet us on a common ground to become bolder, braver, and better personally and professionally.

Our life lessons have provided the opportunities to experience emotions and achievements that are:

- filled with passionate energy and love
- charged with powerful struggles
- and followed up with action and breakthroughs

This brings us full circle. We were the players and coaches, who are now mentors and advocates. We invite you into a strategy session that will add value to your life, your results, and your higher levels of success. The fundamentals we will lay out to you are rooted in experiences we've had in life that have blossomed into keystones of who we are and how we do business.

When you connect with the stories we share, you'll gain a strong understanding of how our drive has made a difference in our lives and we will guide you to uncover the same for yourself.

PURSUING THE GOAL: HAWLEY

Team building is essential to the success of any team. The 1991 Arkansas State Volleyball Team was no exception. What could be a better opportunity than to go to a teammate's house on the lake? Boating, waterskiing, and swimming sounded like a great time to be had before the preseason started. I still have a picture of us on the boat that day. It reminds me of how young and happy we were, the last bit of summer bliss, before I got a call that changed everything.

The call was from my brother. At first, I was shocked that he even had the right number to call; it was the 90s, so everyone's information was more than just a few taps away. This was the first clue that something was wrong. My suspicions were confirmed by the end of the call; bad news was an understatement. This day meant to be filled with joy and team bonding was the day that I was told my father was dead.

I was in utter shock by the time I had hung up the phone and I was convinced I had heard my brother wrong. It wasn't my dad, it couldn't be. My mom was the sick one in the family; he must have meant Mom, not Dad. My mom had struggled with multiple sclerosis for a long time. By the time I was fourteen years old, she was in a wheelchair and her symptoms continued to get worse with each passing year. It was a monster that had seemingly been eating away at her. At that moment, I felt like it had won.

Grief instantly consumed me. During my flight back to California, everything was a blur. I had no idea what I'd heard or said since the call; all I had was this persistent aching in my heart, brought on by the knowledge that my father was gone. So, twelve hours later, when I got off the plane and my sister picked me up, I was in disbelief when she quickly confirmed what my mind attempted to hide from me: it was indeed my dad who had passed away.

How could this be? I wondered. Just a few days before, he had been eagerly awaiting a trip to watch me play in an early season tournament.

From the already jarring and tragic change to my life, I had been thrown onto a new breed of pain. I thought about so many memories of my dad, like his love of sports and family; how he would cheer me on; how we had always been my biggest fan; how we always played the same lotto numbers, knowing one day he'd hit it big. I remembered how he always encouraged me to be my best and told me I could do anything I set my mind to do, how he was a jokester and always had something sarcastic, yet inspiring, to tease me about when I was home from school. Not anymore. Dad would never see me play volleyball again or be my pillar when I needed it.

More urgently, my dad would never carry my mom to bed again. He would not be there each night to help her into bed or help her rise every morning. He would not be there to take her fishing, with the special fishing pole he made for her so she could still fish with him. He was gone now, so who was going to be Mom's primary caregiver? He had taken care of her for thirty years, and had been her caregiver for fourteen years of their life. He had done this without any complaints, only with love and dedication. Now, someone else would need to take over; my mother could not live alone in her condition. But who could?

My brother was only seventeen. My sister, although several years older than me, already had her hands full with two toddlers. This left me. Should I leave Arkansas State in my senior year to go back home and assume the role of caregiver for my mother's sake? My coaches wouldn't have faulted me for going back to California. No one would have. My mother was not pressuring me, and everyone seemed to be leaving the decision fully up to me and I agonized over it.

After tearing myself apart over this decision, the final factor that would help me decide came from an unlikely advisor—Dad. Three years prior to his passing, my father had quadruple bypass heart surgery. Before going into the operation that he knew could mean the end of his life, he had written a note for each of his children and his beloved wife. Having survived the surgery, he did not give us those notes after it. I only discovered them right after his passing while we were going through his journal and personal effects.

In his note to me, he mentioned how proud he was of me for being the first person in our family to go to college, how he was inspired by my ingenuity to figure out how to be good enough at volleyball (and softball) to get my college education paid for, and to be able to travel all across the country to play. This was my answer. This was Dad telling me to go back to school and make him proud. This note gave me the permission I needed to finish what I started. It helped me decide to follow my intuition and go back to Arkansas to complete the volleyball season and graduate from college.

With this newfound fire and Dad looking out for me from above, I went back and put everything I had into finishing both school and my senior season.

We ended up winning our conference and went on to play post-season at the National Invitational Tournament. We were conference Champions, 41–8. It was a great season for the team and an even better way to finish my college volleyball career. The decision to return to volleyball after the devastating loss of my father changed my life. If it wasn't for that note from my dad, I would have never gone back, and my volleyball career would have died with him.

After graduation, a tough economy led me back to the University of Arkansas for my master's degree and the opportunity to be the volleyball team's assistant coach. This was another decision that changed my life for the better. Though it started as a practical choice to make myself a more marketable asset, it ended up shaping me even more into the person I was meant to become.

Coaching has taught me so much about volleyball and life. As a player there was a love for the game, but as a coach I have learned to appreciate every aspect of the sport. Volleyball is complex, from the starting whistle to the match point. I learned the beauty in every intrinsic part of the game. My role as a coach became a fundamental part of who I am, first in the gym, now every day in my business. Still, the success of my team continues to be just as important to me as it has always been… Coaching has taught me true leadership.

Today, I look back to those two decisions I made and see that they have become pillars to my success. Knowing that, Carey has her own story of how important decisions shaped her life and sculpted her into the person she is today.

PUSHING MY LIMITS: CAREY

Welcome to small town America. When I say small, I mean we were considered a village. The eighty-five students in my graduating class were the product of two villages put together. There were horse buggy signs on the sides of streets and every business was a local mom-and-pop shop. That was where I moved during my freshman year of high school. I was a transplant in the middle of a school year. Everything was different. I knew no one.

We competed in Class C (against other small schools) for sports. I adapted to an environment that was like its own little planet. To me, it all seemed new and alien. I was a cog thrown into a machine that was already warm and humming. It was a daunting change to make at fourteen.

My love of sports was the easiest, most reliable bit of familiarity and introduced me to a group of potential teammates and coaches. Since I had arrived toward the end of basketball season, I had one choice—try out for the junior varsity team. After a successful run with JV, I was moved to varsity for the playoffs. That happened in a few short weeks and while it felt great to be catapulted to varsity, that fast-tracked progression rubbed a few in our small community the wrong way. Despite what anyone else thought, I decided I wanted to prove to them and myself that I was a rightful pick for varsity, so, what I lacked in developing fast friendships, I replaced with dedication to our team.

Sports became a mechanism that I would later use to hoist myself up into a university that was otherwise financially unavailable to me. I plunged myself into athletics, which, at that level, came naturally. At that time there wasn't much pressure for me because the pool of competition was small. My teammates and I did well, and despite our athletic success, I was unsure of whether I could compete at the national and collegiate level. I kept working hard though, putting in my time, facing challenges, training, practicing, and sacrificing.

Eventually, I did start to receive recognition locally and on the state level. I tried out for and made a high-level volleyball team that pulled players from around the US to compete in Europe. By my junior year, my efforts paid off. I received several scholarship offers to play both basketball and volleyball at the collegiate level, but Northwestern stood above the rest. A smaller campus, prestigious academics, situated just north of Chicago, and a Division 1 school in the BIG 10 Conference? All my boxes were checked.

Northwestern wanted me for their volleyball program, both for my skill and height, as I am blessed to be 5'11". This made me appealing for the setting position. Thankfully, at that time in volleyball, a shift was happening. Coaches were acknowledging that tall setters provided a blocking advantage. So, the coaching staff offered me a full athletic scholarship. Bright-eyed and eager to take this stunning opportunity, I accepted it, not fully aware of how much I would have to overcome.

Shortly after the initial euphoria wore off, I started to face the reality of what being a college-level athlete meant. That's when the fear crept in. What if I wasn't good enough for that level? Small town to big city, and BIG 10 Northwestern… it seemed impossible. Could I even handle the physicality? Was I prepared for the academic rigor? Despite my fears, anxieties, and the what-ifs, my faith, my drive, the support of family, teammates, and coaches, I found something greater than fear. So, I took the leap.

When two-a-day practices began, I found myself entering with a different energy than anything I'd faced before. Facing the fear dead on, I stepped out of my comfort zone and onto the court, resolved to meet the challenge of my next step.

The true nature of college volleyball became apparent at one of the first morning practices. We had been doing intense conditioning and two-a-days for less than a week. I was so sore, I could barely bend down to tie my shoes. The senior outside hitter, who happened to be a BIG 10 Honorable Mention for her stellar play, was across the net from me. I was down the line on defense, feeling the burn from all those workouts in my legs. Still, I readied myself as much as I was able. When someone like that gets a perfect set, makes the perfect approach, and gets perfect contact with the ball… there's only so much you can do. She slammed the ball down the line, hitting me square on the forehead. The difference in the speed of the game was jarring from what I'd known, even when competing internationally. This is what I'd been afraid of. This was what I had resolved myself to take on. This was college volleyball and getting annihilated by a perfect swing was just my friendly introduction to it. Talk about facing your fears!

Regaining my composure from being blasted by this seasoned veteran, I looked to my coach for wisdom. And what did he have to offer? "Welcome to college volleyball."

That was the beginning of what I would have to push through, and I knew it. It was a cumbersome task, not only because I had finally gotten smacked (literally and figuratively) with the true intensity of collegiate volleyball, but because on top of the physical challenge, there was the added struggle of being thrust into a big city, knowing no one. Not to mention that the academics at Northwestern were the most challenging I'd faced. All this was tied to the full scholarship I received, which was integral to the whole operation because we likely could not have afforded a private university education any other way.

My preparation came via trial by fire. I was thrown into the deep end and fought to learn how to swim amongst all the things threatening to weigh me down. Sure, I didn't want to let others down, but mostly I needed to prove to myself that I could handle the incredible opportunity I'd been given.

I used every resource I could. I prayed a lot. I listened to motivational music. I ate healthier than I ever had before. I received "extra" repetitions. I stuck to a strict regimen. It took an "all in" mindset to prepare me for the court and the classroom. It required sacrifice, humility, a competitive investment, and a substantial amount of self-development. The comfort zone wasn't an option. Neither was quitting. My most important struggle to overcome was getting over my fear and to stop feeling like I didn't belong. This could only be done by facing those feelings and pushing through anyway.

Good news! I did have success. I earned the opportunity to start my freshman, sophomore, and junior years. I battled through injuries and made it through. I graduated in four years. These experiences created lessons to guide me in life and are exciting for me to share with you.

FEEL THE FEAR AND DO IT ANYWAY

It's okay to feel fear. Recognize it for what it is: a reaction to stress. Often fear is false evidence appearing real. You take the step forward, shoot the ball, give the speech, make the phone call, or address the conflict, regardless of the fear. You do it anyway. Try to embrace the fear. Sense it. Look it in the eye. It does not define you. It is not a real factor holding you back. Fear is, like most other temporary roadblocks, part of a mental game you play when reaching outside your comfort zones.

Work hard to practice standing up to your fears. These moments when you choose to confront your fears will build emotional maturity. When you exhibit emotional maturity, you will be able to see through fear and perceive the objective facts of a situation. When this happens, it is because you were resilient and strong and refused to give into the fear or anything else that stood in your way. This book will require you to do these things to help you in your commitment to realize amazing, well-earned successes in your life.

No matter how you approach it when you get there, you become self-driven and aware of what needs to be done. This is, in part, the emotional maturity component that allows you to embolden yourself to believe you CAN do what you set your mind to accomplish. You replace the "can't" or "won't" with "can" and "will." A simple change of language in your self-talk can mean a world of difference. Instead of telling yourself what not to do, say clearly what you are going to do. Instead of "don't let fear get in your way", tell yourself "Rise above the fear to get what you need to do done." Put positive actions into your goals and thoughts and use positive language with those around you. Focus on what you need to do rather than what you don't want to do. Make getting results a priority rather than eliminating faults.

A positive mindset that helps overcome fear is a choice. It is a choice to remain positive when you are faced with failure and resistance. There are going to be times when you fail or are disappointed in yourself, others, or simply the situation. This is when you need to choose to stay strong and keep your head up. Even going into a new situation, you first must look objectively at the possible outcomes and accept both the good and the bad, knowing that you are going to stay positive and deal with it either way. Swallowing fear and choosing to persevere is the definition of courage. It will take you to wonderful places in your life that would have otherwise been unattainable if you had backed down.

You will miss 100% of the shots you don't take! You will not get 100% of the promotions or sales you don't ask for! Pause and really think about these statements... Meditate on them. It's fear of failure, of mistakes, or sometimes the pressure of success that gets in our way just before we would accomplish our goal. If we had just pushed through and taken the leap anyway, we might just have made the shot, received the promotion, met the person of our dreams, and achieved the next level of success we sought.

In the business world this is particularly important because you are going to thrive and rise above the rest by your willingness to do the things that others avoid. Learning the nuances of this is at the heart of emotional maturity. Recognize this in yourself and others and help them see past the fear. Finding ways to keep going will change your perspective and give you the needed push.

PLAYBOOK STRATEGY

Let's work together to discover where you stand now and start the process necessary to outline your ultimate success playbook. How do the concepts and stories we share fit with the goals you have? You'll be strong in some areas, less so in others. We're here to help you uncover your strengths and determine the aspects of your life that need improvement. Identifying these strategies will help you grow, develop resilience to conquer life's obstacles, and become a well-rounded individual capable of achieving greater success than you ever have before.

We don't just want you to learn another perspective on growing better in life. We want to give you concrete steps to implement positive change. We believe those who immerse themselves with diligence and consistency in this work are the ones who benefit most. You do this by:

- Determining your current baseline
- Outlining what you desire to get out of this experience
- Taking definitive action toward your goals
- Making a commitment to yourself and your accountability partner(s)
- Reviewing your results and adapting to progress and pitfalls

By the end, you'll have developed your ultimate success playbook to start pushing through your fears. Are you ready? This book captured your attention for a good reason, so it's time to take your first steps into a better, more successful you.

Recall the moments in your life where you made critical decisions. Think even to decisions you made that seemed trivial in the moment but ended up having a huge impact. Trace the trails of tiny choices that have built your life to where it is now. Decisions equate to change. Big or small, they add up and can make all the difference.

In Chaos Theory, there is a concept called the "butterfly effect." The butterfly effect is based on the power of decisions. It suggests that even something so soft as the flap of the butterfly's wing can lead to a hurricane down the line. What wings have flapped in your past and created storms in your present? For both of us, the decisions we made—appearing smaller at the time—have set us on the path we walk down now. For Carey, making the leap from small town varsity teams to the sole starting setter on a BIG 10 volleyball team opened the door to a new life. For Hawley, the choice to return to college after the devastating loss of her father allowed her to finish school and go on to have a successful career as a player, coach, and businesswoman. Those were defining decisions that completely shifted the trajectories of our lives.

However, not every decision is going to be the right one, and you won't always know how they'll turn out. Decisions leave us with an unknown variable for our future; that's the risk of life. We're asking you now to make the choice to be vulnerable and open up to the process. Absorb the information we're offering to create a personal playbook that can help provide guidance throughout your life.

YOUR TAKE-AWAYS AND THE DAILY PUSH

The following set of principles are the foundation of our ability to push through to the other side of obstacles that previously stood in our way:

- Practice (Practice, Practice, Practice): Discipline, time management, and hard work
- Perseverance (Just Keep Going): Persistence and resilience
- Growth (Rise Up): Confidence, courage, and humility
- Organization (Keep Score): Strategy, accountability, and adaptability
- Cooperation (The Huddle): Teams, teamwork, and success
- Strength (Fierce!): Assertiveness, aggressiveness, and competitiveness
- Actualization (Triumph): Leadership, self-reliance, and execution

These fundamentals build upon each other, just as they would if you were training in a sport. In order to spike the volleyball, you must first learn your footwork, arm swing, timing, and more. Once you achieve competency in one area, challenge yourself to take the next step.

Each chapter will have an exercise for you to complete. We call it The Daily Push. These exercises are designed to help you rewire your current narrative to a stronger one. Each exercise will build upon what was learned in the previous chapter. Move forward once you've completed the activities. They will make your journey more successful and your progress more impactful!

You may be wondering, is this just another book filled with information about what you should do but haven't done? Absolutely not! When the steps are completed, you will have created a valuable resource far too few people have access to: a customized playbook that outlines how you can exponentially grow as a person and achieve the goals you know are possible with the right mindset and action plan.

If you're committed, we are honored to be a part of this process with you. This is a book for developing those who desire a winning strategy for their best life possible.

Are you ready to push through to the next level personally and professionally? We're ready when you are.

FROM US TO YOU

"Today, do what others won't so tomorrow you can accomplish what others can't."

SIMONE BILES

A MESSAGE FROM CAREY

Have courage to speak up and use your voice. Much of the fuel for my voice stems from my mother. She often felt conflicted and hesitant about expressing her perspective. Mom encouraged me and I honor her memory and lean on her spirit for courage. It's only when we believe in and commit to the actions necessary that our journey begins.

May our work together help you push through the obstacles previously in your way. Face your fears of the unknown outcome and do it anyway! We are all on different journeys, but your home court advantage can be this book and journal. Use them for brainstorming, as a safe place to be vulnerable, a place for "aha" moments and inspiration, and a place to write down the actions you commit to take.

A MESSAGE FROM HAWLEY

Strength and courage are divinely interwoven in the fabric of my life and journey. While my relationship with my father was one of admiration and closeness, I realize now as I look back at the life my mom lived that she taught me so much about who I am today. My mom was one of the most courageous people I have ever encountered. She battled much of her adult life with a devastating and debilitating disease. She did so with love in her heart, a smile on her face, and joy for the little things in life.

This book is a tribute to all the lessons I have learned from her and my father, as well as countless others who have helped shape my life. Sports have taught me how to be many things, including coachable, accountable, and hardworking, and to have a passionate and competitive attitude. I learned mental toughness from watching my mom endure years of massive physical limitations. A task as simple as scratching your nose is easy for a healthy person but was torture for my mom. That type of cognitive wherewithal has given me years of strength and emotional intelligence to pull from.

Leadership is not for the meek or weary. True leadership is having the fortitude and characteristics to handle a situation with grace and glory. Every human being on this earth will be faced with tough decisions during their lifetime. May this journey you embark upon give you the strength to face those choices head-on. My hope is that this playbook will be what inspires you to have your breakthroughs and growth.

Pushing through is something we all must do to get to the best of what life has to offer. Together Everyone Achieves More (TEAM). In this book, we are your coaches, teammates, trainers, fans, and cheerleaders. Let's accomplish something meaningful and bring out the champion in you.

PRINCIPLE #1: PRACTICE, PRACTICE, PRACTICE.

"That wall is your mind playing tricks on you. You just need to say, 'One more step, I can do this. I have more in me.' You'll be so proud of yourself once you push yourself past your threshold."

KERRI WALSH JENNINGS

Everyone starts off at square one. Whether it's a child learning to ride a bike or a new executive learning how to run their first business meeting, we all start in an inexperienced place and are prone to making mistakes. So how do we improve? How do we stop fumbling around in the dark and start becoming skilled in whatever it is we're trying to do? The answer is practice. Most people know that age-old adage "practice makes perfect." Well, that's not always true, but practice will certainly create proficiency.

For us, as athletes and as businesspeople, practice is essential. However, it is a product of something more complex than just practice that enables us to enact new behaviors and skills.

1. Identify what it is you want to improve upon or what skill you want to gain. What is going to make you an asset?

2. Break that skill down into its basic parts. What does this skill require you to be able to do?

3. Practice each part of that skill, building competence before moving onto the next. For example, if you're trying to be better at running meetings, you would need to first improve your public speaking, organizational, and leadership skills (to name a few), before you can excel at running a meeting.

4. Once you're competent in each part of the skill you're trying to learn or improve, it is helpful to receive feedback to know how you can further improve. After you've received your critique, you can use this advice to fine-tune what you're doing until, finally, it becomes almost automatic.

Doing all this takes commitment, discipline, routine, and hard work, all before you see your accomplishment. You must make an active decision to change and follow through with an action plan. Part of this plan needs to include a structured schedule that provides a guideline and a focus for reaching your goal.

As college athletes, we learned the value of routine because it was all we knew. Our respective teams were tight ships that only ran so well because we followed the schedules that our coaches outlined. They structured time for warm-up, practice, lifting, meals, travel, matches, and everything in between. Our academic advisors worked with us to schedule our classes and helped us stay on track to graduate in four years while working around our practices and games. Every part of our days was laid out for us, and it made us learn the value of time, discipline, and structure. Everything was accomplished promptly, with little time to waste.

In grad school, we were the ones who took ownership of setting schedules for ourselves and our teams. When we became entrepreneurs, taking control of our schedule and using the routines we learned in college became a foundation for our success. Now as coaches, professionals, and businesswomen, our schedules matter more than ever. We put in the practice and structure for the success that determines our results.

A SCHEDULE WITH IMPACT

Preparation is vital to your daily routine. Whether you are accountable to a business partner, manager, or yourself, the consequences of following through with your schedule matter to someone. You need to create a schedule that allows you to accomplish all the tasks that must be done every single day of your workweek, and perhaps your weekends too.

Hawley, for example, gets up in time so she can exercise every morning to start her day. This usually means she is up at 5:30 to 6:00 A.M., depending on when she meets her first client and if she needs to be ready to walk out the door. She understands the value of ensuring the discipline of her daily routine. So, even if she had to get up at 4:00 or 4:30 A.M., she would do it to ensure her routine remains consistent.

Key Point #1: "Opportunity does not waste time with those who are unprepared." -Idowu Koyenikan
Make sure you are prepared to start your day on your best terms and with the right mindset.

Carey learned these critical lessons from the summer before she left for Northwestern. She was provided a workout routine with a gradual build-up to help her be prepared physically and mentally. From nutrition to exercise to sleep, nearly every minute of her days were accounted for with time blocks. Her calendar was specific and filled to the brim with essential tasks and routines. That summer provided a journey of transformation that allowed Carey to start her freshman season strong and created the discipline of executing a planned schedule.

Key Point #2. Lombardi Time—Vince Lombardi (Great Coach of the Green Bay Packers) expected his players and coaches to be 15 minutes early to meetings and practices. If they weren't, Lombardi considered them late.

Be at least 15 minutes early for scheduled activities and appointments. Many leaders use this as a litmus test for the level of commitment of their athletes or employees'. Meetings may start or the entry door may be locked 15 minutes prior to the scheduled times of meetings. If you're not early, you can't attend.

Think about having an important meeting with a client. He has a million dollars to invest. The crucial appointment is set for 10:00 A.M. on Saturday morning at a nearby coffee house. The client shows up at 9:45 A.M., is shown to their table and waits. His clock has started; 5 minutes goes by…10 minutes…15 minutes, still you have not arrived. Finally, you arrive at 10:10 A.M. How does the million-dollar investor greet you? Do you think he will be signing over a check to someone who is late? The answer is most definitely NO! The thoughts going through his mind are not on the product you're pitching; they are lingering on your tardiness and spawning questions in his head. Will you be late for other meetings? Are you going to be late when the product needs to be delivered? What about when it's time to pay him? Tardiness is disrespectful and often signals unreliability. Employers, investors, dates, coaches, and anyone else in your life will catch on if you are continually late.

Key Point #3. "**Time isn't the main thing, it's the only thing.**" -Miles Davis
Use your calendar effectively and efficiently. Use time blocking throughout your day, week, month, and year to outline the different aspects of your schedule and put yourself in the best position to execute your plan.

Hawley adheres to a rigid schedule, waking up every morning a minimum two hours before her first appointment. It is critical to maintain her routine so she can set herself up for success. Her day starts early to accommodate 20-30 minutes of quiet time and prayer, then, she exercises by riding her Peloton and stretching, ending each workout with pushups and sit ups. After that, she gets ready for her day.

When she was commuting from San Diego to build her office in Orange County, CA she would often rise at 4:00 A.M. because she knew she had to leave the house by 5:15 to miss traffic. This routine is what has always driven Hawley's success and kept her busy life running smoothly.

Time blocking means scheduling the activities in your life that are important for your success. Personal time, travel time, exercise, important appointments, training, evaluation, and planning time should be booked in your calendar and color-coded.

These key points allow you to learn what to expect from your days. Practicing a routine every day allows you to accomplish tasks automatically, leaving space for mastering what you are doing. Acting on these fundamentals is a winning strategy.

MAXIMIZING EFFORT: CAREY

Coaches use drills to teach and develop fundamentals. As players become competent at the basic part of a skill, other drills build upon the foundational aspect of a skill to enhance execution and likelihood for success. The Pit Drill, although difficult, demonstrates this.

In volleyball, the Pit starts with one or two players on the court with a coach, plenty of volleyballs, and all other players collecting and handing balls to the coach. The coach will hit, toss, or tip (approach the ball as if to spike it but instead gently push it with the fingertips in order to deceive the opposing defense) a ball far outside the reach of the player. It is virtually impossible to touch, let alone dig off the ground. If the player makes a solid effort for the ball, the next one will be hit, tossed, or tipped a little more playable. It might be a few inches higher off the ground or closer to one of the players; still difficult, but less impossible.

The player or pair of players earn a point if they dig the ball before it hits the floor, or if the second player is able to touch the ball before it hits the floor after the first player has kept it up. This continues until the player or duo achieves 10 points. If a player gives up or does not make a valiant effort to dig the ball, the next one will be thrown across the gym or hit far away from the player.

What is the point of this drill? Our coaches used it to teach us to try to touch any ball, no matter how seemingly impossible. The only chance you had to get a point was to try your best. If your teammate dug or touched a ball, you did not want to let them down. As the season wore on, the Pit became part of our team culture, and the attitude we took with us to the court during practice translated to our matches. Surviving the Pit challenged each of us to attempt to run down, dive, or get a fingertip on a ball that appeared out of our range. We repeated that drill over and over and over throughout the years.

That "nothing hits the ground" mentality and effort translated into action during our matches. It taught me that even when odds seem impossible or something appears out of your reach, give your best effort and you may get the ball, win, or achieve your goal.

EXECUTING ON THE FUNDA-MENTALS: HAWLEY

Carey has identified how we use the routine or practice and drills to build on each other in the athletic situation. Now, let's take a look at an example from the business side. As I continue to expand a team in my insurance business, I constantly seek ways to support them in daily improvement.

Recently, I extended an invitation to the 24 people on my team who are ready for promotion to their next level within our company. For them, this promotion offers a leadership position. To be eligible, they need to have a certain number of people on their teams who have earned a certain number of commission dollars. I was excited about this, as these results are great news for everyone. So, I sent out an email to those people, sharing my calendar link and giving the opportunity to set up a 30-minute planning session with me. In this session, we would reverse-engineer their numbers to see what numbers they would need to achieve in the next 90 days to keep moving toward their leadership goal.

I was able to work with about half of the individuals who were in the position to move to the next level. During the planning we look at the numbers to determine their per deal commission amount. Next, we look at their calendar, then determine how many appointments they need to run to close a deal. Finally, we look at how many people they would need to meet with to schedule enough appointments to close x-number of deals to help them hit their commission goal. While it seems elementary, many people forget to go back to the basics when they are seeking to achieve their goals.

Business professionals need to reassess and adjust their strategies based on their numbers just as teams need to practice after a game. Finding a coach or a teammate that can help you assess your Point A will support you in moving closer to your Point B. For my team, there is also the component of teaching and training others. For this metric we look at their current team and how those individuals perform. Making sure we have the right people in the business is another key strategy that requires constant analysis and reevaluation. Along with this, we always look for people who would be suitable for our business. These people must be coachable, accountable, and hard-working.

As an entrepreneur, it is important to understand how to determine what routine will create a successful schedule for you. Knowing your numbers and understanding accountability matter greatly (accountability is a principle we will discuss later); however, self-discipline and practice are what will make you outshine the competition.

PRACTICE PAYS

There are some people born with the innate desire to achieve their athletic best. However, not everyone possesses this desire, nor the talent needed to follow through. You hear about the great athletes and their work ethic, how much and how often they practice, how young they started, and how they fell in love with the sport they played. They usually had a parent who thrived in sports and pushed them to have a diligent practice schedule and mental toughness.

Las Vegas Stars point guard Kelsey Plum is one such person and her story of practice is inspiring. She offers a great example to follow on how you can practice your way to being one of the best in your field, and for people who want to play strong at a high school, college, and even a professional level, she exemplifies the results you can achieve when you never stop working toward your goal.

Hawley is a family friend of the Plums, so she had a chance to view Kelsey's regimen. Even as a fellow athlete she was impressed with what she saw.

When Kelsey was a child, she was always playing basketball in the backyard. The court became a second home for Kelsey and she was always doing something: running, shooting, practicing free throws, practicing passes when someone was available to step in, and challenging others to try to beat her with certain moves.

Every action she took was focused and had a purpose. From a young age, Kelsey was driven to be the best possible player she could be. She knew she wanted to play at a collegiate and one day professional level. She set goals and showed a striking determination for accomplishing them, even as a child. That passion and resolve has carried her into a successful career as a professional basketball player, shown by her status as the number one pick in the 2017 WNBA draft.

This practice discipline is often something that comes at a young age and is based on your willingness to do something others won't or can't do.

What Kelsey did in sports is what you can do in life, personally and professionally. Do something that will set you apart from the rest. Maybe that means a greater commitment, putting in that extra effort, or going out of your way to do something difficult that will inevitably produce better results.

Regardless of who you are, discipline is the key.

4 LESSONS IN GOING THE DISTANCE

The point of practice is to learn how to execute and make the skill automatic. Whether it's individual or team practice, each step you take will bring you closer to your desired outcome. These are the lessons that have helped us reach our potential, benefiting us both individually and as members of a team.

Lesson #1: Complete the set
When you are working to set appointments, going the distance to make the necessary phone calls, or knocking on that one extra door is a part of the practice. You must dig deep to finish what you started. Push yourself to complete your commitment even when it is difficult. Even when you don't want to, even when it's late and you're tired, or you'd rather do anything else.

Doing things that you've committed to do, regardless of the internal and external obstacles will build resilience, and it is part of the process of becoming a better, more reliable person.

Let's say you're at the gym. You've set out to do five exercises, five reps, five miles on the bike, etc. Whatever you've set out to do, you've made a clear goal for what you want to accomplish and are committed to accomplish it. You get down to business and finally, you've finished four out of the five parts of this workout. You're tired, sweaty, you feel like you're going to crumble into a heap on the floor. This is when you learn exactly what you're made of. Are you going to tap out and give up when you're so close? No one is holding you accountable except you. It's time to decide whether or not you respect yourself enough to adhere to your own commitments or if you're going to give up. Now is the time to push through. You can see the finish line up ahead. It's only one more…and not only will you finish, but you will have done exactly what you set out to do.

It is worth persevering through even seemingly small or insignificant goals because when it comes down to it, your ability to follow through is a matter of grit and self-respect.

Lesson #2: Scouting
Identify the individuals that have accomplished what you are working to achieve. Be aware of what they are doing differently and emulate the activities that set them apart. If possible, seek out their advice.

Athletes learn how to apply the lessons of those who came before them in meaningful ways. The same is true in careers. When we noticed the same skills being practiced by both athletes and successful businesspeople, it offered us insight into what success truly requires: discipline, routine, time management, and hard work.

The realization of the similarity between business and athletics connected the dots for us. We noticed how various aspects of sports, like hard drills at practice, were required for parts of business, like training and joint casework. We realized structure, perseverance, and discipline are crucial, whether you're on a court, field, or in a boardroom.

Lesson #3: Pregame Warm Up
Define what your day is going to look like and then actively pursue it. Make a personalized plan that lays out what you need to do for:
- Your morning and nightly routines
- Preparing for a client meeting
- Getting ready for an interview
- Putting yourself in an alert and prepared state of mind so you can adapt to whatever the day may bring.

Time management is essential. It's easy to lose focus in the many distractions of today's world. When you stick to a routine it demands your attention, constantly. At times, you'll get the unexpected; an urgent conversation, a personal text, a workplace dispute that needs handling, or a technology problem. When this happens, you must find the discipline to get back on track as quickly as possible. Become aware of distractions and refocus. Stop procrastinating and prioritize. Set a deadline and work to complete your task on time. If you work in an office, consider closing your door and putting your phone on silent, do not disturb, or even turn it off completely. Maybe go to a library where it is quiet. These are all steps you can use to get back on track and stay on task.

Lesson #4: In System
Once you've set your routine, time blocked and color-coded your schedule, properly prepared for each aspect of your plan, and practiced, all that's left to do is execute. When you begin your day, your daily plan is laid out; you are prepared for what needs to get done. When you apply the right dedication and focus, few things can stop you. Routine, discipline, habits of success, and the drive and willingness to work hard will help you make the improvements you are setting out to make. If you get off track, use some of the previously mentioned strategies, or discover one of your own, to get back into your routine as quickly as possible.

GETTING BACK ON THE FAST TRACK

Is it possible to give 100%, all the time? We admit it: sometimes we are not disciplined in certain areas of our days or lives. We get off track and don't follow our routine. The question is, when you fall off track, what can you do to get yourself back on schedule?

Only you know when you have not achieved what you set out to do. If this happens, the best thing to do is catch yourself and get back on schedule. How you do that is up to the support and structure you have set up in your life.

When you find yourself in the position of not being on track in any capacity, remember to keep your personal commitments. This builds confidence, which is a wonderful trait to help you stick to your routine and commitments. The progression of a drill is meant to build up a player. The same is true in business. If you are building one skill, it supports you in growing into the entrepreneur you want to be. All these things work together, and so do all the principles we are going to share with you.

THE DAILY PUSH

Preparation is what you need most to plan for a successful day, every day. Today, you are going to start doing this. If you already prepare for your workday before it begins, you can review this information and see if there is anything you can tweak to enhance your results.

Here's what we need you to do:
- Grab your schedule, whether it's digital or paper
- Slate out time for any appointments you have scheduled for tomorrow
- Now fill in the gaps between those appointments with your urgent priorities, the things you want to get done, and those items which are low priority
- Fill in urgent priority tasks for times when you have your best energy
- Continue on, filling in non-urgent tasks and then low priority items

Here are some helpful tips to guide you:
- Do not overbook yourself. Remember you're practicing for success, not burnout
- Consider doing your top three priorities the night you organize them

- Get a solid night's rest so you wake up with energy and desire to achieve what your daily goals are
- Prepare this schedule from your own perspective, not how we run our days (we all have different needs and daily objectives)

Reflect on your routine and how you manage your day. How can you make it better? Are you going to put a reminder on your calendar and set aside time for something? What will it take to accomplish your goals?

To help gain momentum in building up your practice routine, list three things you will prioritize so they have the required time on your schedule. Use the table below or grab The Daily Push Journal.

Task	Time Given	# of Days/Week

You need to own your schedule and take responsibility for it. Make it work for your goals. How you decide to execute it will determine if your practice is working or if you need to adjust your approach.

Also, make sure you start doing this step before diving into the next principle, which focuses on the importance of persistence and resilience.

And last, take a breath and appreciate this life for the opportunities it is giving you!

AN INTERVIEW WITH KELSEY PLUM

Our chance to interview Kelsey Plum was a wonderful opportunity, especially for Hawley, who watched her relentlessly practice basketball as a child. Her hard work and commitment to all areas of her success are paying off in the life she leads today. Kelsey played her college career at the University of Washington. By the time her senior season ended she had won every award available to a NCAA women's basketball player. These awards included the 2017 Naismith Trophy, the Wade Trophy, and the coveted Wooden Award. Kelsey was the number one pick in the 2017 Women's National Basketball Association (WNBA) draft, a starter for the Las Vegas Aces, and an inspiration to young people who wish to follow in her footsteps.

What is one story that has had a major impact on your career?
I remember one of my most difficult times was when I got to the University of Washington to start college. Before I was ever on the court, I was named team captain. This put me in a situation where I was asked to lead a group of women who already had a history with the team. As for me, I didn't

even know where class was. I had not yet earned their respect. I was told I was the kid who was going to change the culture, starting right now.

At eighteen, you do not know what that means. You think you can do it, but you really have no idea what is involved. So, for me, having to learn how to lead a group of people was a great challenge. As women, we do not easily warm up to other players on the court or even play hard for someone else. I had an uphill battle, filled with trial and error. It took me two and a half years to reach a point where I did connect well with players of all different backgrounds and the culture of the program began to shift.

How has that example fueled your success?
I think my experiences helped me learn that any situation I am thrown into, is one I can manage, whether it is overwhelming or holds a lot of pressures and expectations. I now have ingrained a self-belief that I can make it work and I am going to thrive.

What do you do daily to help pursue your goals?
I learned that it's necessary to write down what I want. This is a big indicator for me as to how badly I want it. When I can see it and put it on paper, I am committed to going for it. Before I start a basketball season, I write down specific goals for myself and the team, so I feel all the details of them vividly.

This also gives me a chance to grow into the type of woman I want to be for my family, siblings, and friends. I pray and like to meditate in the morning, as it gets me into a joyful perspective. Then the day begins, working on everything basketball related that I must do.

How was the jump from college to pro basketball?
This remains an ongoing process. Nobody really writes you a road map for decisions along the way. This last year I have built better relationships with Sue Bird and Diana Taurasi, which have helped me immensely. They have a vast amount of knowledge and can help me sort through questions such as, where were you at this point in your career? What country should

you play in? Should I look to get traded? I rely on women like these two, along with faith and prayer, to guide me. You can call family for support and they care, but they do not know the business.

I have made mistakes and learned. Someone shared this with me the other day: "Whatever decision you make is the right decision. Make it and go." I take this to heart because I cannot stress about what I should have done or could have done.

What message do you have for someone who wants to get into the elite mindset?
Humble yourself. You do not know anything, so do not try to pretend you do.

Be patient. It will not come as quickly and fast as you want. When you think something must happen now, you lose out.

Never lose the drive that made you start. This is true in sports, business, and all of life. If you lose that love, what do you have?

Of all the awards you've won, what is the most meaningful one you received?
In high school, at the McDonald's All-American game, I won the Best Teammate Award. At the time I did not appreciate the magnitude of the award. Today, as an adult, I understand how important it was to be voted best teammate by my peers.

Another honor that is personal to me was the monumental experience of winning the gold medal with the US championship team in the summer of 2019. As a young girl I could only imagine and visualize playing with Sue Bird and Diana Taurasi. When the opportunity came it was a dream come true. Maybe someday I will be the woman to inspire girls who are playing AAU today.

PRINCIPLE #2: JUST KEEP GOING!

"Make up your mind that no matter what comes your way, no matter how difficult, no matter how unfair, you will do more than simply survive. You will thrive in spite of it."

JOEL OSTEEN

Perseverance is essential to growing and reaching your goals. You must have an unrelenting will to keep going throughout your journey. There will be times when you are faced with overwhelming obstacles. You will run into roadblocks, conflicts, and make mistakes, but it is vital to press on, no matter what comes your way. This means working your way through challenges as they occur and supporting others in their own pursuit of success. Perseverance is required to achieve the next level in whatever you do. Without it, people tend to settle for mediocrity or give up when the going gets tough. Yet, it is the endurance that drives you past the halfway point and on to true greatness. That is why you must push through when you feel resistance; the fight is worth the prize.

It isn't always easy to keep going, but it is necessary. Failure and mistakes are part of the journey, especially when dealing with a new challenge for the first time. You may begin to feel hopeless, discouraged, or pessimistic about your efforts. This too can be an essential part of the growing process. Just as a lotus flower must fight through the mud to bloom, you too will have to struggle for your success. To reach a breakthrough, you must work through the breakdown. Pressing on through hardship will not only help you grow and succeed; it will also teach you how to deal with resistance in the future.

Typically, it's limiting beliefs, pain, or fear that hold people back from the results they are seeking. Negative self-talk often results in a mental block that can prevent people from reaching their full potential. When you notice yourself or those around you getting trapped in these cycles of pessimism, you must step in, eliminate those patterns, and turn them into positivity. These moments plagued with self-doubt and negativity are opportunities to grow and help yourself and those around you conquer limiting beliefs. It requires you to connect with the emotional maturity we have said you will need. This is the source of much of the strength you need to do all the things required of you, even during the most challenging times.

This is something Hawley learned firsthand as she made her way through a painful and difficult situation.

PAIN DIDN'T STOP ME: HAWLEY

Summertime in Bakersfield, CA means the temperature can hit a blistering 114 degrees and I was in the middle of one of these summers. I was 14 years old and had the best plans for the days leading up to high school. My best friend and I had matching Aero Scooters. Although my family had rules about how to be safe on the scooter, I was a teenager who was more interested in having fun than worried about getting hurt. The safety precautions were to always wear a helmet, long pants, closed toe shoes, and no passengers. After finally persuading my parents to let me go on a long ride with my friends, with shorts, sandals, and a friend in tow, we planned out the day. It would be a ride to the yogurt shop for a sweet treat and soda.

The ride to our destination was uneventful. After that, my friends and I decided to get our drinks for the ride home. We started racing as we entered the street where my best friend lived. This is when the fun quickly ended.

As we were speeding along, my passenger leaned one way and I leaned the other to avoid the ice our friends had thrown our way, then splat, we contacted the pavement. Pain was inevitable; however, shock took over and I jumped up and convinced myself and my friends, "Don't tell my dad." I had softball practice later that day, and the truth set in as my friend's mother pointed to my leg and said, "I don't think you will be playing any time soon." It was road rash, all down my leg. Not only had the asphalt shredded my leg, but since we had been going so fast when we fell, the wound was also a burn. When I went to the hospital, the doctors had to dig the pebbles out of my leg with a razor.

Fortunately, nothing was broken, but that didn't make what was left of my leg feel any better.

From my ankle to the middle of my thigh was a massive abrasion, more of an intense burn from the heat. My face had two raspberries awfully close to my left eye. I also tore up both of my arms, which included hands and fingers with the same painful road rash burn that encompassed my leg. It would take weeks of care and physical therapy to heal my leg, arms, fingers, and face. I could not allow that to get in my way. I had been selected to the All-Star Softball team for the league I played in and had to prepare for the tournament.

The summer of '84 was full of plans, including the All-Star tournament. To get back in shape and be able to play, I had to endure pain that I had never felt before. Once the first few days had passed, the plan for recovery was laid out to me. If I wanted any chance of playing softball this summer, I had to overcome some mental blocks and physical limitations. I had to run every day and that meant after each workout, I had to go home and redress my wounds. Every time I moved, my abrasions would reopen and bleed, but it was something I had to endure if I wanted to be in the right shape to play in the tournament.

The perseverance to keep up with my training was one of the greatest challenges of my life. I remember my dad driving next to me while I ran. Well, running isn't exactly what I'd call it; it was more of a slow hobble doing a poor job of imitating a run. While I was struggling to keep in shape, I had an area all set up in the house to do physical therapy that would help my wounds heal.

A fan blowing cool air onto my burned leg was a frequent companion that summer as I watched the 1984 Olympic Games. The USA Men's Volleyball team was amazing to watch. The grit and determination of these athletes inspired me and paralleled the kind of athlete I was attempting to be through that ordeal. Although the All-Star team I was working hard to play for was by no means Olympic, it was still the big leagues for a 14-year-old and an absolute honor to be a part of. I was introduced to visualization and its benefits to athletes for the first time while training for this tournament.

After a long summer of cleaning and dressing my wound, applying ointment, and hours spent parked in front of the TV with that fan blowing on my leg, the tournament finally came, and I was ready for it. The tournament ended up being an incredible experience. Not only was it a unique and thrilling event to be a part of but it was also a phenomenally successful one for me as a player, especially considering the grueling weeks beforehand. I started off the first game in the third inning with a home run. During that same inning, I hit a triple and had 4 runs batted in (RBI's). After the victory, I learned that the home run I hit was the first ever for a girl from the Plaza Bobby Socks, the team I was representing. All the suffering and perseverance paid off and the results of the tournament were more than worth the struggle. All of this proved to me that I was capable of persevering through adversity and coming out the other side new and improved.

Long before I even knew what it meant, situations like that summer were sowing the seeds of emotional intelligence in me. Over the years, facing resistance has continued to change me for the better.

Despite all the physical trials of that summer, the real struggle was the mental battle it took to prevail over my inner limitations. It was a constant labor of emotional strength to get through the pain. Each morning for weeks, I would wake up to excruciating pain, knowing I needed to nurse my wounds and push myself to stay in shape. I never would have made it without the right mindset to conquer it. I had to do this every single day for nearly a whole month. The determination and resolve to do that came from emotional maturity and a strong desire to win.

Today, the resolve I gained that summer carries over into both my personal and professional life. The same ability to dig down and move past resistance persists. I pride myself on my ability to operate effectively during emergency, crisis, or tragic situations, especially in business.

In all situations, I keep these perspectives with me to help push through all situations. It makes a difference. Just like Carey's story has impacted her in both life and business.

DAY OF THE UNDERDOGS: CAREY

Coaching club volleyball was an opportunity I was excited to tackle. One of my most memorable seasons came after several elite players left to form their own club. This was unfortunate at first, but it ended up teaching my team and me some lessons which outweighed the loss of those players.

It all began at try-outs, where we ran drills and competitive situations to select players based not only on talent, but also intangible skills such as heart and willingness to fight. The girls who tried out for the team were considered underdogs from the beginning since they had been in the shadows of many of those top players who left; winning had not come easily for them before. To rise to the level they were shooting for, they had to dig deeper and work harder than even those that had been on the top team. They had to push themselves more than they ever had just to level the playing field.

We started out the season in a power league. A power league is a group of teams who play each other throughout the regular season, then are ranked based on the outcome of those games for the postseason tournament. In the Chicagoland area there were two ways to qualify for the USA Volleyball National Tournament (USAV): you can go to a qualifying tournament and finish in the top two or three, depending on the qualification for that year, or you can finish in the top three or four of the Windy City Power League (WCPL).

Our team decided to compete in the WCPL to try and qualify for the tournament. Over the period of several months, we were doing middle of the road at best. Heading into the final weekend of the qualifying tournament, we had to win all our matches to qualify.

While we knew what we had to do, the teams ranked above us also had to beat each other in just the right sequence to allow us to advance. Every factor had to fall perfectly into place if we were going to have a chance to qualify for nationals. It seemed almost impossible at the time. We were a team of underdogs leftover by the splitting of our club. Although we had come such a long way and had melded together to become a great team despite the meager beginnings, this was a huge task.

Throughout the season, we had incorporated visualization into our practices and tournaments.

Visualization became a key component to our routine and had been integral in molding us into the successful team that we became. We brought in a mental performance coach who specialized in visualization techniques to help both me and our team get in the zone.

Understanding that most of the game is mental, we knew it would be one key to our success to enter that tournament having visualized exactly what we wanted to achieve. So, as with all other tournaments, at the beginning of each playing day, we would circle up as a team, lock arms at the elbow, and go through these steps: close our eyes and belly-breathe several times to relax, set our intentions for that day and for the game. We imagined stepping into our circle of power/confidence, and vividly imagined the goal/intention successfully and joyfully completed and then replayed the desired outcome at least 3 times. The culmination of this routine was our visualization of victory.

Together, we would stand, eyes closed, and imagine the moment we had finally won the last match of power league and qualified for nationals. We focused on every detail of the scene; what we heard and saw, how we felt. We felt that adrenaline rush that would wash over us when we won. This was one of our secrets to success. We had seen our triumph, now we just needed to make it happen.

We won all the matches we needed to win; we had done our part to get where we wanted to go. Now, our fate was out of our hands. In volleyball leagues like this, the outcome of a team's season might not be wholly up to their record. The system that decides who qualifies often makes those selections based not only on how a specific team performs, but also on how the teams ranked above them perform. So, the other teams in our league would decide if we qualified or not. Thus far, all of the right teams had won or lost as needed, and by the end of the weekend we were in a tie with one of the teams previously ranked above us for the final spot to qualify for the USAV National Tournament in Dallas, TX.

The tournament that seemed to be stacked against us became the tournament that gave us a chance. We had to scratch and claw and fight every step of the way. Then we had to play a tiebreaker on top of everything else. Sometimes tie-breakers are a single game to 15 points, but since the national tournament was riding on this one, we played this game to 25.

It was neck and neck. The momentum of the match kept shifting back and forth between the teams. Other than that, it's hard to recall. I was so focused that it seemed like everything I did, every correction, direction, and change I made, was on autopilot. Our players were in sync with each other and performing at their all-time best. All those years of experience and our mental preparation made that match almost instinctual. I do remember, however, that we went on to win that set 25-21. I have an awesome picture of the aftermath of that game, with the score in the background, my girls screaming with excitement, some on their knees, some jumping in the air, fists clenched as they cheered for themselves and each other. They were consumed by the overwhelming joy of their monumental victory.

This was everything they had sacrificed for. All the workouts, practices, tournaments; every lesson learned and tear shed. All the floor burns, bruises, and sore muscles had led them right there, to the center of that court, reaching for each other in celebration of a well-won war. It was exactly how we had imagined it repeatedly. They already knew how it would feel, because they had felt it before during our mental preparation. We had visualized this moment, and it had finally come to fruition. For me, it still stands as one of the proudest moments in my coaching career. Knowing that I helped them get to this point, despite all that threatened to subdue them, still motivates and reassures me to this day.

We could have given up anywhere along the way, but we didn't. Instead, we persevered and stayed focused on one match, one set, one point at a time. We were a competitive, resilient bunch, and we leaned on each other, believing that each of us would achieve what we had been working toward all season. Those girls had grit and determination, and no one could tell them otherwise, especially after that qualifying match. I am so proud of them still, and I hope they continue to be proud of themselves for what they demonstrated that day.

I tend to believe that underdogs have an edge when it comes to emotional maturity because it is built from situations like this. As their coach, I aspired to help them build strength, physically and emotionally, and show them that they could rise above their circumstances and anything else that got in their way. Visualization proved an incredible tool that allowed us all to make our goals a reality. Even now, though I have left the court behind, I find it is still a valuable practice for both me and my team.

THE GREAT VISUALIZATION

One strategy that can be used to help you persevere through adversity is visualization.

Visualization, or mental rehearsal, means vividly imagining the experience and the results you want. Immersing yourself in your possible future success can provide guidance when you feel lost and hope when you feel hopeless. We believe that this technique can be incorporated into your life and help to rewire limiting beliefs.

In Carey's case, visualizing the desired outcome of a match, tournament, or even their season, played an integral part in their victory. Carey and several of the players on that team hardly remember anything about what happened that final weekend of power league play. It was as if they were functioning automatically, without having to really think about their movements or reactions. What they do remember is that winning moment from the picture taken at the end of the match. This and many other achievements happened in large part because of the consistent, repetitive visualizations the team participated in every practice and tournament day. These rehearsals allowed them to enter the zone.

What is "the zone?"

A state of ultimate focus. Some describe it as a vortex of incredible energy where you are on autopilot working to achieve your goal with no distractions. It's as if there is no time and space and nothing physical or mental in your way.

One way of reaching the zone is to visualize the results you're seeking. To effectively visualize, vividly imagine your own moment of victory. Then go beyond just seeing and feel it with your whole body. Pay close attention to your heart rate, your body's chemical response, and your energy levels. A successful mental rehearsal makes you feel euphoric and invincible. You may also feel a sense of excitement, drive, and a feeling of reward for the accomplishment. When you experience what it feels like to achieve what you are striving for, your brain doesn't know the difference and works to make your mental rehearsal a reality. You are training your subconscious mind to see what you visualize as real.

3 WAYS TO KEEP YOUR GOALS MOVING FORWARD

The challenge is to find that inner strength you need to keep going when things seem to be at a standstill, or so tough you are thinking of not moving forward. Keeping yourself going is one of the most admirable steps you can take. You will find you are able to grow stronger and more confident with each repetition.

1. Discover your flow state

This is a part of being in the zone. The flow state is something an athlete experiences when they get into the zone and do not remember much about their game or race. It is such a clear tunnel vision that the only thing they see is the desired outcome. Your body is on autopilot and you execute all you have practiced and drilled to perfection.

In business, the flow state happens when you set your sights on an objective or goal that helps you excel to the next level: the new target you are aiming to achieve. Everything falls into place with your presentation, your appointments, your closes, your interview, and your professional growth.

2. The greatness lies in the breakthrough

Breaking through your challenges requires persistence. Catch yourself at the point of facing an obstacle and keep going. As previously mentioned, the breakthrough is often the result of a breakdown. This can be personally or professionally. Whatever situation you're in, a complete resolution is necessary in order to move forward and have a breakthrough. Ask your coach or someone you respect to push you. They know you can do what you may not feel you can. Allow them to stretch you, help you expand your thinking, and show you ways to push through to that next level.

3. Become "unstuck" from the middle

When you are in the middle of a challenge, it is often hard to see where you are and sometimes even realize that you're stuck. You can move beyond the impediment with a coach or somebody who can help identify why you're stuck and inspire you to persist. Contrary to what some may think, people do not have to achieve what they set out to do all alone. Rely on your coaches, mentors, teammates, managers, friends, or spouse.

These guidelines, when you practice them and apply them in your lives, will most certainly improve your results.

THE DAILY PUSH

In this Daily Push, we are going to work with some things that you may have put on the back burner or never completed due to something holding you back. Sickness...life events...a busy schedule...a mundane task in the challenge. All these things contributed to you falling short of achieving what you were meant to do. You need to remember that the seeds of these ideas were planted in your mind for a reason.

It's time to move onward and stop spinning your wheels. Let's start with this identification exercise. Feel free to use a notebook or receive more insights by using the Daily Push journal.

Step 1:

Identify and write down up to three goals or times when you met with resistance and stopped progressing on a goal or objective. Remember what it was that veered you off course and identify what happened in the outcome.

Step 2:

Replay those situations you recalled. Now rerun each video in your mind and change the outcome. Visualize what you want to see, feel, and hear. Dive into this with as much detail as possible. For example, if your reality is that you got cut from a team, visualize all that you would be doing to have made that team. You must understand these details to rewrite the narrative in your subconscious mind. Repeat this exercise several times for each of the situations. Mentally rehearse the new outcome and how you feel. Celebrate your promotion! Feel the adrenaline from scoring the winning shot. Listen to the laughter, engagement, and fantastic feedback from your presentation.

Step 3:

Write down your visualizations in as much detail as possible, either in a notebook or The Daily Push journal. Do not use a computer—take your time and indulge your senses. Include every marvelous detail of the visualization and how it has impacted you. This is the best way to have it come to fruition.

With these three steps complete, you can start taking action to keep moving forward. You must have an action for all this thought to work.

Another exercise that is fabulous to do, but requires at least one other participant, is one Hawley did during a corporate retreat. Those who could do it found a boost to their confidence which led to great accomplishments.

First, find a person who can assist you. This is also a great time to start looking for an accountability partner, which will be discussed in the chapter "Rise Up."

Now, take one of your unaccomplished goals and visualize achieving it. Try to break through a piece of paper or a thin piece of wood that someone is holding for you. If you break through it, you have a mental image which can set you up with the fortitude and diligence to achieve what you've set out to do. If you don't break through it, don't worry.

This means you must strengthen your belief in your visualization. Keep practicing it and then try again in a week or two.

The best way to keep going is to already see yourself on the other side and what it feels like to have accomplished what you previously thought was unattainable.

AN INTERVIEW WITH KARCH KIRALY

We were honored to catch up with US Women's Volleyball coach, Karch Kiraly. While we were growing up in the 80s, Karch was impacting the volleyball world as a four time All-American, three-time NCAA National Champion at UCLA and as a crucial member of the US Olympic Men's Volleyball team. He was an Olympic gold medalist in 1984 and 1988 indoor, and 1996 on the beach. He took the time to share stories, philosophy, and insight to guide us all.

Out of your life experiences in volleyball, share one that has had an impact on your life and career?
In 1996, the inaugural year of beach volleyball in the Olympics, my partner Kent Steffes and I were across the net from Mike Dodd and Mike Whitmarsh. We were in a hard-fought battle and earned the gold medal.

Three weeks before the end of the 1996 season, my shoulder gave way and I had to have surgery. As I healed and began to compete the following season, my level of play plummeted. I would swing at the ball and it would end up five feet off the mark. The architecture in my shoulder had changed and I grew really frustrated. My new partner Adam Johnson and I were having a terrible season and essentially all of it was because of me.

The 1997 Milwaukee tournament led to my biggest frustration yet. We were eliminated by 8:30 A.M. on the last day. I had let my partner down and my shoulder didn't seem to be improving. We had won so little prize money that I didn't want to pay the change fee to fly home early. Instead, I drove around Milwaukee and found a bench on a quiet beach. I sat down to reflect on where I was and where I would go. I had a heart-to-heart meeting with myself.

I had to accept that I was not going to be the player I was before. The old Karch who played gold medal volleyball seemed to have disappeared. It seemed inevitable that it would be my last season. I had put so much pressure on myself the past year and had failed both my teammate and me. I had enjoyed a great run for over 20 years, but it was time to let go, and make peace with that.

Then something strange happened. Once my expectations were lowered, my level of play improved. The following weekend at the next tournament, we won. Then we kept winning. We won four tournaments in a row.

When I removed the expectations, I was able to achieve more peace of mind. This allowed me to have less pressure and less tension, along with more forbearance and grace to myself. This was a powerful experience that shifted my mindset and the actions I took afterward. I was eventually able to return to a similar level of play, and I ended up getting the privilege and bonus of competing ten more years in the sport.

Once you removed pressure and expectations, everything changed. What happened next?

Once I became more patient with myself and built gratitude for the "bonus" time, things changed for the better. I no longer feared the end of my volleyball career. That peace of mind certainly helped my performance, and the joy I was able to derive from it. Some of our USA Women have gone through similar challenges and have also found some success through lowering their expectations and raising their patience.

How do you use this in your life and coaching today?

Reading *Happiness is a Serious Problem: A Human Nature Repair Manual* by Dennis Prager was another influence on my approach toward expectations. The book used the Buddhist concept that expectations can lead to great unhappiness.

For example, if I am healthy and go in for my annual physical, it's easy for me to expect a clean bill of health and continue taking my good health for granted. If instead I hear the doctor say, "Whoa. I don't know what that is. We'd better get it checked out," that can quickly get my mind racing toward worst-case scenarios. It can also force me out of any expectations for good health. If I find out after several tests that it was nothing, I'll wake up the following morning with a much greater appreciation and gratitude for the same good health I was taking for granted just days earlier. I no longer "expect" to wake up with good health each day, and I will cherish it more, have more gratitude for it.

In volleyball, I try never to go into any competition with an expectation of a certain outcome, no matter how strong our team is. I can have high hopes for our team to have a certain outcome and can know that we're capable of a certain outcome, but I try hard not to expect that outcome.

I find that when I deny myself expectations of a certain outcome, I can make myself work harder for it. If instead I expect a certain outcome, I can't squeeze the same level of effort out toward that end.

What do you do daily to keep this practice active?

In all areas of life there are tons of strong opponents out there. Every time a team takes the court, the enemy has a real say in the battle. Our US Women's Volleyball team is really strong we're the #2 ranked team in the world. And yet, the other high-ranked teams are so strong, so the matches are close. A hard-fought match might end with each team having won 100 points. Understanding the fine line between winning and losing, it would be a mistake for us to enter any match expecting to win—a mistake to take that result for granted.

Knowing how thin those margins are, we must accept that every minute of our work is critical, every minute counts. And there's a cumulative effect at work, where all of those minutes, all of our efforts, all of our actions, add up to who we'll be and how we'll compete when we step on the court. Our competition is out there working hard too. So, we have to make the most of our precious time together and use it to swing a small margin our way, so we can win 101 points, and they take 99. This can be the difference between an Olympic gold medal and no medal.

PRINCIPLE #3: RISE UP

"You may encounter many defeats, but you must not be defeated. In fact, it may be necessary to encounter the defeats, so you can know who you are, what you can rise from, how you can still come out of it."

MAYA ANGELOU

What challenges are you facing today? Whatever they may be, confidence, courage, and humility are crucial to overcome almost any roadblock in your way. This is not easy, yet each time you take a step forward, take decisive action, and give your all, you put yourself in position to push through. You build confidence each time you work through what previously stood in your way, even when it is so tough that you are considering turning around or quitting.

Even when a situation seems out of your reach or impossible, rely on yourself and believe you will rise up and work through those times and they will lead to improvement in your life. Work hard to demonstrate confidence over insecurity, courageousness over cowering, putting your best foot forward over mediocrity, and humility over arrogance.

One resource to help you rise up to all you face in business and in life is an ally. An ally is someone you respect, can learn from, and desire to emulate. These people are critical in developing strong qualities to help you learn to get through any situation coming your way. A strong ally can be female or male, are not egocentric, have similar experiences to what you are now confronting, and can be an accountability partner in your success.

Allies enjoy success in their lives but not at another's expense. These people are encouraging and direct. They push you while also keeping you in check. Often thought of as mentors, these individuals help you understand your actions better. They question you when things seem wrong, provide feedback, and inspire you when you need it most. They understand the importance of a person's emotions, while not giving you a pass to have emotions rule your decisions. This creates an important question for all of us: how can we use our emotions to take an effective stand when it's necessary?

Hawley offers a great perspective on this.

THE COURAGE TO TAKE A STAND: HAWLEY

In the fall, I was in Las Vegas at our corporate office for a committee head meeting. I was attending as the head of the Technology Committee, and it seemed like a routine meeting. It was intended to serve as a check-in to make sure all the committees were on the same page and performing their duties to align with the company's overarching goals. My meeting went well; my committee was on track and functioning effectively. However, another meeting caught my attention—the Executive Leadership Committee. It was my observation of this meeting that turned this trip from a standard check-in to a catalyst for a lot of introspection about inequality in business.

To give you context, I am at the highest level of leadership in my company, with the title of Managing Vice President (MVP). We used to have an MVP committee that met several times a year, but by the time this committee head meeting rolled around, I realized that the MVP committee hadn't actually met in months. I was told on this trip that this new Executive Leadership Committee was the replacement for the MVP committee. I happened to observe one of these meetings in motion and was shocked to discover that there were about a dozen people in the conference room, yet there was not a single woman among them and truly little diversity. This struck me as odd, especially since our company sales force is wonderfully diverse and has approximately 45% women, which is atypical in the insurance industry. Clearly, something was off.

As a high-ranking woman in the company, I felt disrespected and outraged. So, I was faced with the choice of saying something or staying quiet and going about my business as usual. After some soul-searching and consulting two respected people for more information, I decided I needed to take a stand. This took courage because I knew my merely mentioning it could lead to disagreement, as well as others not agreeing with my actual observation.

Talking to the person heading up this committee meant standing up to a good friend of mine; his wife is one of my best friends. We have spent time traveling together and our kids play together on company trips as well as celebrating birthdays and other benchmarks in our life. When I talked with the leader of the committee about it, I was filled with some animosity—after all, I am deeply passionate about equality for women and diversity in the workplace. My irritation toward the situation was visible to those in the meeting. He noticed I was spirited on this topic, as I explained how our company was remarkably diverse, nearly half women, and that our Executive Leadership Committee did not demonstrate this.

In our conversation I was told that many on the committee were pro-women, but what does that really mean? It certainly does not mean that they can think like women or make decisions based on how we think. It doesn't mean that they will promote women or diversity to the field. I brought up that we spent five years cultivating the women's initiative and this is the respect we get: being left off an executive committee. The status quo in insurance companies was playing out before my eyes. At the end of that meeting our CEO pulled me aside and told me he had my back and that the diversity issue would be addressed. I knew that bringing it to his attention would help in making the change.

I did it; I voiced my viewpoint strongly. It wasn't eloquent or polished, but it was real and direct, and I am proud of myself for taking a stand that day. What I really saw with this situation was an opportunity to bridge the gap: to create a more inclusive environment to bring out the best qualities in everyone. This is what I strive to do as a leader: to place the entire team on a winning trajectory. There is no room for egocentricity in cases such as this.

Confidence and courage often come with a price and you need to exercise caution. In this case, I also gave into gossip and bad-mouthing my colleague during some of the business trip's downtime. Prior to addressing this situation, I was not talking fondly about the person leading this committee. I was quick to judge and point out his perceived faults. Although I had addressed the situation with him, I didn't let it go. I kept pushing every chance I got with any executive that would listen. I kept on pleading my case and in doing so I lost sight of my values. I am not proud of myself for this behavior.

That night I did not sleep very well. I knew that gossiping and attempting to get others on my side by talking behind someone's back did not demonstrate the professional fortitude with which I should have handled the situation. The next morning, as I went through my workout and quiet time, I knew what I must do. I owed this man an apology for gossiping behind his back. Even though he didn't know that I was doing that, and he might never find out, I knew it only diminished my character by not addressing my challenges directly with him. When I did address him the next morning, I apologized for talking behind his back and for not coming directly to him with my issues. I also told him it would never happen again. I did not know then what I do know now: that my relationship with this person has grown to a new level. I have a greater appreciation for him and who he is as a leader in our company.

I am also happy to report that now things have changed. We have more diversity, including several women serving on the Executive Leadership Committee. Although the confidence and courage it takes to express a concern felt challenging, speaking up has made a difference in the well-being of our company.

I've learned that good leadership isn't a gender or a color; it's qualities you have which help everyone achieve better for themselves, which also benefits the whole team. We all must stand for excellence, fairness, and diversity to become better. Women and men do think differently, which is why in order to support the entire company you must have a well-rounded view of what is happening in the field. When the field has a large minority represented, leadership must include a diverse point of view so we can serve our people best.

Passion can be expressed in many ways. For women this can stir up some emotions and at times those might be challenging to men. When we started the women's initiative within our company, one of the priorities was giving the women a place to be heard, without judgement and allowing for emotions. This one thing helped our company grow tremendously. My hope is that one day the people in our company realize how fortunate we are to have an extremely diverse sales force. Industry events have always had conversations about how to attract diversity into our industry.

The final point I want to make is that this is not a battle of women against men. It never has been. Life and business are a joint effort. Our company can thrive when we work together for the betterment of those we serve. Our company mantras of "we help a lot of people," "we create life changing wealth," and "we get better every day," are shared amongst a group of diverse individuals and reach across the country. Great leadership is required to benefit us all, not just a handful of people. Let's rise up together.

A great example of this comes from Carey's powerful story of courage to do something different.

THE LINE: CAREY

The line. People hang their reputations, their careers, and even sometimes their lives on it. Putting something on the line means putting whatever it may be at risk. You could lose, fail, or get hurt by taking that risk, so it takes immense courage to put something "on the line."

In sports, athletes often put their bodies on the line for the success of the team. Football players collide on the field, divers flip and twist inches from their platforms, jockeys are a misplaced hoof away from rolling under a 2,000-pound horse at break-neck speeds—risk is a core tenant of athletics. However, body parts and safety aren't the only things on the line. Sometimes it is a reputation or career or even our own pride and dignity.

As a setter, I went out in front of a gym full of spectators to play a game against some of the best volleyball players in the country. I was a small-town kid defending with every move I made, as well as my right to be on that team and at that school. Professionally, I put my dignity on the line when I step in front of a group of people for a presentation. What if I make a mistake or embarrass myself? I put my pride on the line when I commit to an ambitious goal that puts my skills to the test. What if I fall short and disappoint myself or my team? I risk my reputation when I make a recommendation to a client. What if it was the wrong one to make? All the anxieties, the what-ifs, are present and real, and that does not mean that I or anyone else don't have courage. Courage means that you take on the challenge despite your fears.

I have found no better sentiment on courage than this quote by Theodore Roosevelt:

> *"It is not the critic who counts; not the man who points out how the strong man stumbles, or where the doer of deeds could have done them better. The credit belongs to the man who is actually in the arena, whose face is marred by dust and sweat and blood; who strives valiantly; who errs, who comes short again and again, because there is no effort without error and shortcoming; but who does actually strive to do the deeds; who knows great enthusiasms, the great devotions; who spends himself in a worthy cause; who at the best knows in the end the triumph of high achievement, and who at the worst, if he fails, at least fails while daring greatly, so that his place shall never be with those cold and timid souls who neither know victory nor defeat."*

In 2014, my husband John and I decided to start our own company. After gaining experience in the field for years and realizing how we wanted to operate within it, we left our previous firm to enact our vision of the potential we saw for ourselves and a future team. We went from being mere underlings who didn't have to worry about anything except our own clients, to paying rent and making payroll, not to mention the liability of owning your own firm.

When we started that journey, there were no guarantees. We could make a wrong turn and end up lost in debt and struggling in such a competitive economy. We had never needed to look after the office or supplies or trademarks or logos. This was a whole new world of things that could go wrong, but we took the leap regardless. We stepped into the roles of leaders and decision-makers and eventually team builders. We had to accept that we could fail and end up unemployed with two children to take care of and bills to pay, but if we succeeded, we would have our own business, led by our beliefs and ethics with a team that we cultivated. If we succeeded, we could give ourselves, our children, our team, and our clients better lives. It was a gut feeling that turned into a goal. So, we decided to step into the arena and fight to make that goal our reality.

We had a meeting with the owner of the firm we were with at the time. We told her that we wanted to conduct business according to our values and vision. After discussing how we could accomplish our goals while remaining at the firm, we realized that our ideals did not align with staying there. This meant our best decision was to find our own space, which we did. Then we packed everything from our now former offices into our minivan and moved out. Thus, TrueWealth Advising Group was born: new location, new logo, and everything else. At first, we weren't sure how we were going to manage any of it. It was like becoming new parents again; we had thrown ourselves into the deep end and now it was time to sink or swim. Thankfully, as with raising our two girls, we managed to keep our heads above the water with this new chapter in our lives.

The decision to start our own business was one of the biggest in our lives and has turned out to be one of the best. We had to be brave as well as trust our ability to handle the situation and whatever obstacles came with it. Today, we have a strong team full of talent and even more potential. We've created an environment that we believe has become the key to our success: one of respect, trust, and cooperation.

This journey epitomizes the courage and confidence it took for us to envision and cultivate our success. We put everything on the line. We wouldn't have done it any other way.

WHAT DOES IT TAKE TO RISE UP

These three key points are imperative to finding your grit and rising to the situations that growth and opportunity are sure to present you.

1. Know your boundaries
Setting boundaries is an essential skill for anyone striving for success both personally and professionally. Ask yourself: what makes me uncomfortable or

unhappy in the world around me? What do others do and say that I disagree with? What do I expect from others? These limits may come from personal beliefs, ethics, philosophies, experiences, or even religion. Once you realize what you're not willing to tolerate and what you expect of yourself and others, you must be willing to communicate your boundaries clearly. These boundaries can be how far you're willing to be pushed, what you're willing to sacrifice to succeed, what you're willing to stand up for, or other limitations that are healthy to set for yourself and your teammates. It takes courage to stand up for these boundaries and speak up when they are crossed. Creating boundaries in all areas of your life, communicating them with others, and speaking up when they are crossed will benefit your confidence and emotional well-being. Setting boundaries is also a sign of emotional maturity, a useful tool when dealing with stress, conflict, and other challenges in your life.

Be clear and give yourself permission to say no. Do this without guilt, fear, or self-doubt. These boundaries must be set and upheld with the utmost commitment, which means not bending them to please others or spare feelings. Communicating boundaries must also be a respectful and understandable account of where you draw your line and why. After all, boundaries are a sign of self-care and self-respect. It creates inner turmoil to ignore and suppress feelings of unease and discomfort. As you continue to practice setting and communicating boundaries, you will gain self-respect and, in turn, be able to ask the same respect from others. This is essential to creating a cooperative environment because it is difficult to respect people who do not respect themselves.

Turn the adage of "treat others the way you wish to be treated" on its head. Treat yourself the way you wish to be treated by others, thus contributing to an environment of mutual respect and cooperation.

2. Rising after a fall

Mistakes, setbacks, and failures happen. The key is getting back up after the fall.

Think about the courage it takes to risk again, to have faith in yourself and to move in a new direction. Without rising from a fall, nothing in the history of the world would have been accomplished. Failure is often a necessary part of learning and becoming a better version of yourself in whatever you do. Figure skaters need to fall, basketball players need to get blocked, baseball and softball players need to strike out. People need to fail and choose to rise again to progress. However, failure can often seem like a shameful, embarrassing ordeal. To move past it, you must remember to do a few key things.

First, remind yourself that this failure or loss in no way defines who you are as a person. Again, failure is simply a part of the growing process, not an encapsulation of all you are. When you feel ashamed or disheartened, try to focus on everything you've done right.

Secondly, you must take in what happened and allow yourself to react naturally. It is okay to feel, so be embarrassed, cry, get mad, and allow your emotions to run their course rather than pushing them down.

Finally, take inventory of what happened to get you to the point you deemed a failure or mistake. Analyze why it happened and what you can do in the future to improve and truly use that failure as a tool to learn. Do not fall in vain.

Make sure to avoid the mistakes of the past and use them to your advantage. Rise from failure with your head up and know that life has just given you another hard lesson you won't soon forget.

3. The right environment

Surrounding yourself with people who possess complementary strengths and exhibit positive values that align with your own, nurtures both you and your team's success. In volleyball, players take on different positions. The short, quick defensive specialist is there to pick up whatever the tall, powerful middle blocker can't block. It is extremely beneficial in a professional environment to have people with diverse skill sets who can teach each other and contribute to the common success of the team. When Carey works with entrepreneurs, she seeks out other professionals who are experts in their field, such as corporate and estate attorneys, certified public accountants, commercial real estate brokers, and business bankers, to provide insight into aspects of the integration of their financial, business, and estate plans. The intangible qualities and differing perspectives provide a unique environment that fosters learning, cooperation, and better results.

Be accountable to yourself to cultivate people who can elevate each other and/or bring in an accountability partner to gain the best results from your efforts.

ACCOUNTABILITY PARTNERS

An accountability partner is someone who helps you be accountable for what you wish to achieve. Accountability partners play an important role because they are a part of your team and a huge part of your success. When you commit your goals to others you are more likely to stick to them, to either achieve or even exceed them. Having other people depending on you and being accountable to them will push you even more to fulfill your commitments.

Once you assess your limitations, bring in accountability partners to hold you to your commitments, make an agreement with them about what you require, and both of you stick to it.

Here are recommended qualities you want an accountability partner to possess.

1. Tough love
This person will not let you off the hook on your commitments and is willing to tell you the truth, even if it is tough for you to hear. You can set some ground rules with this person before they agree to the task. This allows the room required to grow personally or professionally without taking a critique personally, but you should take it to heart if you want to improve. It should be someone you respect and trust to commit to, be vulnerable to, and a person you know will take a stand if and when it is needed to get you on track or nudge you to push through.

2. Likableness is secondary

When you are in the moment, facing a roadblock, an accountability partner focuses on your goals more than being liked by you. You give them permission to be tough when needed. These people often become some of your most trusted allies.

3. Directness

An accountability partner will be direct. You must be willing to address someone when they are being vague or non-responsive. If you know someone is going through a rough time (i.e. a personal loss, unsuccessful business or a job), when you approach them about how they are doing, a great accountability partner takes the time to listen sympathetically. You allow them time to process, but you also help them identify steps to move forward. The more direct those steps and the swifter the process time, the faster the person can move forward.

4. Understand your goal

Your accountability partner(s) need to understand your goal(s) and what it will take to accomplish them.

5. Be encouraging

The best coach or mentor knows when to be tough and when you need encouragement.

6. Find someone with shared values

You want your accountability partner to have similar values to you because that will help them be effective and because their actions have proven their worth for the position. They have earned their credibility to call you out and get you back on track when needed.

When you find someone, who can support you with these six characteristics, you've found a golden ally to have in your corner.

THE DAILY PUSH

Have you risen up when life has gotten tough? What has been your response to difficult challenges, bad news, mistakes, roadblocks, or disappointment? Reflecting on this is the first part of this chapter's Daily Push.

Take time to reflect upon the times when you have put yourself on the line and faced difficult challenges. Yet, once you committed to it and connected with your inspiration you were able to push through and see it through to completion. Write down these situations. Make sure you are vivid in the description and bring that moment back to life. Include who you looked to for inspiration during this time. Perhaps it was the author of a book with a significant message for you. It could also be a coworker or a mentor that you sought out. It could have been an accountability partner or ally.

Using the inspiration from your prior success, what steps did you take to keep going? Even if it was small, it is helpful. Now apply these to a time when it could help you become a more confident or better leader. Whatever is out of balance is something you need to identify. Know where your strengths lie in this area, as well as where you are at a disadvantage. Some examples are: if you're low on confidence you'll want to work on gaining confidence in those areas, or if you spend more money than you should you want to start documenting your daily expenses so you can see where to make adjustments.

Discover what actions are necessary and commit to them. Make them part of your normal routine. There are few things more powerful than when you rise to an occasion, not because you have to but because you want to. As Robin from Peloton (*Cycle company*) says:

"I don't care how many assistants you have or how big your team is, you cannot delegate the discomfort it takes to get to the next level."

This is true. You must go through that personal growth yourself. You aren't able to delegate it or have somebody else go through it for you. You need to go through whatever those limitations are. You must figure out what they are and make them a strength for you to be more successful.

PRINCIPLE #4: KEEPING SCORE

"Accountability is the glue that ties commitment to the result."

BOB PROCTOR

High performers do not accept mediocre results, because they have a clear idea of what they want to accomplish and why that accomplishment is so important. They have also considered the minimum requirements for success, as well as the desired outcome. This is the target they set for themselves before pursuing the necessary changes.

Using these minimum requirements as a springboard, you are creating an ideal sequence of events that will lead to your accomplishment. Knowing what you should do to perform the best, as compared to how you are performing, will determine if you are doing a great job, an exceptional job, or if improvement is needed.

This is keeping score. Being conscientious of that score will impact your results and help you know how to make the most of them. It will also help you recognize how your game plan strategy/accountability, your decisiveness, and your adaptability to changes in your plan are progressing. Each of these elements are linked to your ability to push through and craft each step of your plan to have maximum impact. You will constantly need to be aware of your emotional maturity to make it through all situations and try to objectively see everything for what it is.

In business, you learn to assimilate to situations so you can become better at your field. With sports, you are measured on being prepared and physically and mentally fit for what is demanded of you. This is something Carey discovered early on in her college career.

TESTING: 1,2,3...: CAREY

When I left home to begin college at Northwestern, I was excited, yet unsure, about this new phase of my life. I had adhered to a strict workout and nutrition regimen the entire summer leading up to our preseason. I had worked hard to put myself in the best possible position to earn a starting spot. When we arrived on campus, we underwent a series of baseline measurements including the mile run, jump testing, height, weight, and body fat percentage.

In my many years of athletics, I never had my body fat percentage measured until… the trainers at Northwestern used calipers to pinch the folds of my skin on different areas of my body, such as the back of my upper arm, front of my upper arm, upper back, stomach, hip, thigh, and several other areas.

After my initial tests were done, we sat down with the coaching staff, trainers, and strength coaches to review our results and outline our goals. We discussed my nutritional protocol and my customized weight-lifting regimen to reduce my body fat percentage. The guidelines required me to drop about nine percentage points.

I couldn't believe it! After all the summer workouts and disciplined diet, I still needed to drop 9%.

To track progress, I faced those calipers every week. I needed to make continual progress to feel a sense of accomplishment and persevere in challenging myself to achieve the ultimate results. We began our road toward that goal by breaking it down into realistic, weekly steps.

I learned that having goals to achieve meant more than reaching just a number. It was a combination of mindset, plan, and adjusting to accomplish them. I remained focused on my objective and thrived on the progress. No one was accountable for my own results but me.

By season's end, I achieved my goal and it was spurred on by the objective feedback from the calipers. It was worth it, as it taught me a great deal about the importance of accountability. Facing those results every week was tough, especially if there was little improvement or a step backward. Yet I began to feel my strength improve and see my hard work paying off; two aspects that showed I was accomplishing my goals with the help of coaches, trainers, and nutritionists. We recorded what worked and stuck to it, while also identifying and eliminating what did not work.

In this situation, the coaching staff, nutritionist, strength coach, and my teammates were my accountability partners. They asked and cared about the areas in which I was struggling and challenged. There was never berating or belittling, only offering solutions.

When you are in a sport like volleyball, the results you seek can be subjective, at best. Despite that, making yourself as fit and prepared as possible is your best first step. After that, it's training, dedication, and mastering your position on the team. Other sports are more precise, such as swimming and track, which have a clock to show you how you are doing. When it comes to business, the metrics of strategy, decisiveness, and adaptability are measured differently, as we learn from Hawley's story.

RESULTS MATTER EVERY DAY: HAWLEY

The great Thomas Wilhite said, "The only true way to measure a man/woman is based on results; results are often harsh and always fair." I learned this lesson as a young woman, and it has sunk in deeply over time. A lot of people are stuck in a mindset that there is always some justification for why you are not creating what you want. I tackled this daily when I worked for a personal and professional leadership training company.

Being this company's Advance Course Manager provided an abundance of rich educational lessons and personal growth opportunities. Every day we had a meeting about results. We would discuss the results from the previous day and set new goals for the current day. Although the previous day's results mattered, they were meant to be used as an accountability tool—a scoreboard. We asked the following questions: What worked? What didn't work? What do you need to do differently? Who do you need to be to create the result?

Creating the mindset for results requires growth. The question I often go back to when the results are not where I want them to be is, "Who do I need to BE to create the result I want?" I must dive deep into those areas that do not serve me well, and consciously make changes that will serve me.

My position of Advance Course Manager taught me more about accountability than any other program or job I held previously. This is where I learned about S.M.A.R.T. goals (meaning Specific, Measurable, Attainable, Risky/realistic, and Time frame) and they have always been a part of my career. The questions I was asked about what worked and what didn't work, I still ponder daily. These accountability tools also allow my team to be goal achievers and accountable to those people in their life that mean the most.

Another successful accountability tool I learned in that position is how important it is to have visual guides or "scoreboards" (white boards with electrical tape) to see the success for myself. It was a joyous moment for me when I was the Advance Course Manager and had a full board of people's names because that meant I shared in all their stories. Even more so was the fact that their images equated to a visualization guide of how well I was achieving my goal. It required me to be accountable for results, not perceptions of what I thought I had done.

The outcome I have from my two years with this company is how important relationship building is in the sales cycle, especially in personal and professional growth. It was much easier for me to work with someone that had shared their story with me than someone who was not open to personal communication. If they were experiencing fear in any area of their life, I could coach them through it. The people who were more closed off tended to fall off the board.

The area director that I worked for was also responsible for my growth. Although he held a high standard in some ways, he had no attachment to the outcome. Yet his approach helped me to create positive results. As I've grown wiser and matured, attachment is less about self-esteem and more about building up other people.

Even today, I use visuals in my office as a constant reminder of their importance and how they work for achieving goals. On my board I have a representation of appointments scheduled, clients' names, what amount the deal is, and the product. This is all tracked, and the results speak for themselves.

When people go into reasons for why they could not create something, I simply remain focused on the results. To change the results, a change of effort and strategy is required. Once again, it reminds me that results are often harsh but always fair.

What better way to create and understand results than to set strong goals for you to act with?

GOALS TO GET YOU GOING

A goal is a target you set out to achieve, but a goal is just a dream if it is not attached to a deadline and action. You should be passionate about what the target is and WHY you want to accomplish it. Remember, the goal needs to be specific, measurable, attainable, realistic, and timely (S.M.A.R.T).

While the goal is ultimately the big picture focus, it is imperative to break the goal down into smaller parts. In Carey's business, for example, they create a business plan for the year, and then break down that plan into quarterly, monthly, weekly, and daily steps. In athletics you would set your goals for the season and break it down into preseason, conference, post-season, and off-season sections. The longer-term, big-picture target is dependent on the creation of shorter-term targets, which are those manageable steps that lead to a much higher probability of achieving or exceeding the goal.

By breaking down your goal into these smaller parts, you set milestones for measuring progress, evaluating what is working and not working, and then take corrective actions when required. Celebrate the accomplishments along the way, but also correct the course to get back on track if you fall short of one of the interim steps.

When you are making positive progress toward your big picture goal, keep going and pushing yourself to build upon what is working. Conversely, when you get behind on your near-term milestones, evaluate what you could improve, check in with your accountability partner, research best practices, and make the necessary course corrections.

In athletics, statistics such as wins, losses, percentages of success, errors, time, etc. are used to measure results. Often, the difference between winning and losing comes down to a minute difference in one of these categories. The execution of your fundamental objectives and the game plan are evaluated both during and after the competition by reviewing the statistics, evaluating film, meeting to review, and outlining the areas for improvement. There are breaks between smaller portions of the competition and even time-outs during individual matches, allowing for the necessary adjustments.

There are many questions to consider if you want a clear picture of your overall goal. What are the fundamentals of the goal you are working toward? How can you break the big picture target into manageable parts? What feedback do you need to adjust? Who will help keep you accountable and provide feedback? Remember, achieved goals are the result of actions, not passive daydreams.

FEEDBACK STRATEGIES

Feedback is a valuable resource for those willing to receive it. You must prepare yourself and be open to constructive criticisms. Our definition of "feedback" involves information about reactions to a person's performance of a task, behavior, or trait, etc., which is used as an assessment and a starting point. If you are not mentally and emotionally prepared for feedback, it becomes less effective for you.

One important component of feedback is that it is neither negative nor positive. Feedback must be looked at as the information you need to adjust your efforts and strategies to be successful. This may include the necessity of developing a new habit or eliminating a habit that is no longer effective for your personal and professional development.

Accountability requires evaluating the progress you have made toward your goal. Whether in playing a sport, building a business, or simply living every day on this planet, feedback is a great way to measure your results. An example could be someone on a weight loss journey. The scale provides immediate information to the individual who wants to drop some unwanted pounds.

We have both been in situations where we provided and received feedback. We do acknowledge that it is not always comfortable to receive suggestions from another person about what would make us more effective. Nonetheless, we need the courage to hear our shortcomings and then take steps toward changing those behaviors and traits that do not support our goals.

Look at the weight loss example again. If the scale isn't moving south, it is easy to get frustrated and not make the adjustments recommended by an accountability partner or coach. However, simply writing down everything you put in your mouth for a week may be the tool you need to see the straightforward feedback. In this case, it might be that you are simply eating too much sugar or too many calories each day. The important part here is being open to receiving feedback, regardless of where it comes from.

When you are ready to be held accountable, you must be willing to adjust what is holding you back or is not beneficial for achieving the results you want. In a professional setting that may mean changing an employee because having the best people in the right positions helps to achieve the desired results. However, if the person you are working with does have the potential, skills, and traits to handle the challenge, then it's a good time to have a heart-to-heart and work out the kinks.

On the other hand, if you are reaching a point where the consequences of someone's actions are serious, then this person needs to fully understand the situation. This also allows you to listen to this person's perspective about their own journey. Some of Hawley's most valuable agents were ones who wanted to quit and just needed direction to get their mindset back on course.

Finally, you might have to let people go, perhaps because they aren't willing or able to accomplish the goals and objectives necessary to move forward. One of Hawley's mentors taught her the concept of, "If you cannot change your people, change your people." When Hawley first heard this phrase, she couldn't understand the significance this would have in her business. It may sound harsh, but making a change is sometimes required for the business to grow.

As Carey has discovered, one difference between successful people and struggling ones is the willingness to see the reality of a situation and, consequently, accept feedback. Unsuccessful people are often creative in their excuses and avoid the statistics, feedback, and results. People who are willing to push through and take ownership of their results will go far. When this happens, feedback becomes a powerful tool that is welcomed.

Hawley is a firm believer that when you don't like your results, the next step is to determine what you are going to do differently. As Albert Einstein wisely reminds us, "The definition of insanity is doing the same thing over and over again and expecting different results." Change what you're doing to get the results you desire. That is how you play the game effectively. You take information and recognize where you are at keeping score, and then you encourage, create, recognize, and help a person adapt to what it takes to find success. But first, you must know the rules of the game.

THE RULES OF THE GAME

What are the rules of the game you are playing? Do you even know? One of the most effective ways to create your ultimate success playbook is to define these rules. In some industries or situations, those rules are defined for you, and that is the case in most sports. Hawley put this into practice when she volunteered for a leadership position in a coaching program at the seminar company where she once worked.

The definition of a successful coach in this program was to support people in accomplishing their goals—all their goals. This included increasing their awareness around the act of enrollment. When mastered, enrollment is a powerful tool in the sales process. Observing people's development is always inspiring. However, it was doubly rewarding when coupled with personal growth they have already benefited from and the process of accepting the challenge of the 90-day goals-setting program.

Clear rules about how to win the game naturally apply to how you succeed in business and life. It lessens the confusion and complications; after all, there are different ways to play the game. Some strategies and rules vary from others. Hawley practices this on a personal level at home. Her young son no longer gets the luxury of a free win from Mom and

Dad. Like when they play the game Trouble, for instance, if his red pieces are at risk of being bumped back to home base, he now gets bumped. When he was younger, Hawley might not have bumped him while she was teaching him how to play. He is required to use strategy and abide by the rules to earn his victories. As a result, her son is learning how to win and how to lose, which is equally important.

Understanding how you are going to be measured is an important concept to develop. This process helps you to gain an understanding of how you are being measured so you can explore your best strategy within the parameters of success.

Game plan statistics in business vary. However, they may include some of the following: return on investment (ROI), budgeting, annual business plan, cost of sale, price per lead and a magnitude of other factors you might measure in your business or personal life. Knowing the rules before you engage in the business or sport or life will save you time and ultimately money.

Clarity is key! Without it, you cannot keep an effective score.

FOUR LESSONS TO HELP YOU KEEP SCORE

Keeping score is how we know where we are—behind, on pace, or ahead of pace—in whatever it is we are doing. Here are four lessons we learned through experience. They serve as key reminders of what it is like to reach a higher level of performance in work, sports endeavors, and life.

1. Failures are okay if you learn from them

When you are trying to reach new heights, you are going to make mistakes and fall short sometimes. As you push yourself beyond your previous accomplishments, there are bound to be failures. Reflect and face what happened. Get feedback from the statistics, the video, the accountability partner, and the mirror. Be open to learning from the feedback and make the necessary adjustments to improve. Embrace the lesson for what it is: a step in drawing closer to your achievement. Absolutely none of us are perfect and we are all on a journey to improve and be in a better position to succeed. Mistakes and failures are necessary steps for advancement but are often stumbling blocks.

Keep in mind that in volleyball, a great hitting percentage is getting a kill or scoring a point 3 or more out of 10 attempts. This means you either don't get a kill or make errors 7 out of 10 attempts. In baseball/softball, a great batting average is .300. In other words, only 3 times out of 10 do you get a hit. Your goal is to increase your likelihood of success and always having the courage to put forth your best effort. Have the emotional maturity and confidence to face the mistakes you make, the failed attempts, and the resilience to get back up after you missed your goal. This time push through what has previously blocked you.

2. Embrace deadlines

Deadlines set the timeline for your goal and provide a parameter for measuring your progress or achievement. Embrace deadlines by using them to break down the timeline into what it will take to accomplish your goal. Use them to provide a set point to evaluate your progress so far and adjust as needed. Work backwards from a deadline to establish the interim steps needed to put yourself in the best position possible to finish the project, turn in the paper, deliver the presentation, or win the award.

3. Coordinate the "big picture" with the smaller steps

Whether it's your goal or an athletic season you're facing, break it down into parts. How both these aspects work together is crucial to your success. Experiencing the vulnerable moments when you measure your progress at each step, builds momentum and provides guidance for the next step. Celebrating your minor victories along the journey pushes you to keep striving for the ultimate accomplishment.

4. Keep score

Athletics are gauged in statistics. Your score is determined by the ERA (earned run average), free throw percentage, time you run/swim your race, your winning percentage, and your record. In the corporate world, we keep score through financial reports, sales, reviews, and insightful practices such as weekly focus sessions. This is where we examine your results from the previous week so you are placed in a position where you can successfully move forward. This is achieved through modification and implementation of updated strategies.

The benefits of these lessons help enhance your career trajectory immensely. Using them allows for you to be encouraged when your month is not what you hoped for, and to be recognized when you achieve what you set out to do. This becomes an opportunity to take on a leadership role.

THE DAILY PUSH

There are a few parts to this chapter's Daily Push. So much is coming together at this point and we are going to prepare you as best we can. These seven steps will help!

1. Identify a project or goal you have and break it down into small parts. Depending on the goal, it could be daily tasks to complete or even weekly or monthly.
2. With this goal in mind, you are going to create a spreadsheet (see example below) with columns as follows:
   a. What item needs to be completed?
   b. Who is responsible for completion of this task?
   c. When it must be done by?
   d. When it was completed?
3. Decide which one, two, or even three accountability partners you will use to help you on this journey of success. Remember, these are individuals who are going to hold your feet to the fire and reject excuses or reasons why you cannot do something.
4. Share your goals, state your expectations, and set ground rules with your accountability partner(s).
5. There is one last thing you do to help support your efforts in this hard work. Find a mirror and take a solid look at yourself.

You know what your efforts have been this far. If you need to give yourself a talking to before you begin your pursuit to the next level, do so, and then thoroughly commit.

Project/Task/Goal	Steps	Who is Responsible	By When	Date Completed

AN INTERVIEW WITH
SANDRA YANCEY

Sandra Yancey is an internationally acclaimed, award-winning entrepreneur, founder & CEO of eWomenNetwork, a five-time #1 best-selling author, Life & Business Transformation Expert for the Emmy Award-winning TV show *The DOCTORS*, producer of the critically acclaimed movie *The GLOW Project,* and philanthropist. Today Sandra leads one of the most successful multimillion-dollar women's business networks in North America. With over 500,000 women business owners connected through 118 chapters, eWomenNetwork produces nearly 1,500 events annually, as well as the Premier International Women's Entrepreneur Conference in North America.

We were delighted that Sandra sat down with us and shared her "Push Through" story during this interview.

What is an impact story that helped define who you wanted to be in business?

The core catalyst for my business as we know it came about eighteen months into its life. I was still working from my home, with my kids young.

One day I was feeling a bit blue—I don't recall why, just the feeling that I was blue. I picked up my landline and was greeted by my mom.

Now I was in a dilemma with my new eBusiness, which I wanted to build up to be a scalable business with equity. Although I wasn't going to be a solopreneur in this endeavor, I felt like I needed to go get another job, plus work with this dream on the side. Only, at my success level, I couldn't really get a job so much as make a career move. When Mom asked me how many hours I already worked, I said about 14-15 a day, usually until 1-2 A.M. Then my Mom commented on how my thoughts of a new job and doing the networking company on the side didn't add up.

Maybe I should put the network on pause for a bit, I voiced. When she learned I was thinking of quitting, she added, "How do you know you're not quitting five minutes before the miracle begins?" It was a huge moment for me, and I couldn't answer. She went on to say that if I was going to quit, I needed to know right away so I didn't spend the rest of my life wondering why. I offered one last retaliation of "I didn't know what I was going to do" my Mom replied that she didn't know either, but she knew one thing: she had given birth to a daughter smart enough to figure it out.

At that moment, I came to realize that I needed someone to believe in me. I had started to lose a little faith in myself and felt so lonely that I got trapped in my "stinking thinking." Seeds of doubt were everywhere, and it was overpowering. I had to move past it.

What is one of your main beliefs about success?
When you think about what you do for a living, you realize that no one makes it alone. Everyone who makes it has a network. I've wished that faith was a "get you out of jail free" card for when you need it. However, every now and again, it can be dark. This is when you need to put down the shovel and stop digging the hole and reach for the ladder instead.

Building relationships was my ladder. These people came looking for me and to help me. I was able to hang on in those critical moments when

I wanted to let go. My business coach was one of these people for me. He helped me to take a much-needed step backward so I could launch forward.

What habits or daily routines do you have?
The first thing I do every day starts the day before. This is the pattern of how I run the company and even do the budget planning for it. This means that every single day I identify my top three important things to be done the following day. Only I can do these things and I don't go to bed until those three things are done. They are unforgivable and must be done that day.

How have you figured out how to work together as a family?
One of my mentors, Robert Deadman, founder of a billion-dollar business Club Corp., came to see me and asked how I was doing. "Great," I said, only I wasn't. He told me I looked like hell and I ended up caving and telling him I was worn out. He said, "The problem with the rat race is that even if you win, you're still a rat." He taught me how to get out of the rat race and shared how to quit living against the clock so you can get clear on boundaries.

I took the guidance to heart. So, I sat down with my kids and had them tell me what's important to them for me to be involved in or share with them. To this day, my son has zero recollection that I was the co-chair of the Scholastic Book Fair. He could not have cared less about that program. What mattered to him was me watching him play football on Friday nights and he remembers this clearly.

Learning what mattered changed my life. I applied it to both my children and my husband too. Because of it, I think our connection and communication is stronger.

How would you guide readers to push through to the next level?
One of the things I am clear about is that all businesses need to have a business model that can scale. I don't teach people to apply what works

for me: people come into the office and we see what their vision is and scale it according to their plans for growth.

As the business growth process matures, you must constantly ask yourself: do I have the right people, and are they doing the right things? I've found that six things give 80% of the results.

1. To grow people, you must always be growing.
Some are excited about this and others are not. I am doing what I love to do and want to grow within the scope of what I do. Others need to find this same drive in their own capacity, because, if they don't, it will impact customers.

2. You need grace for managing transitions to help you get ahead of the game.
What are your priorities? Get up close and crystal clear on priorities. As CEO, you should only do the things you alone can do. Don't waste your time and talent, because this will slow down—even halt—growth and stop you from getting ahead of the game. Measuring metrics matters and it is tied to priorities. What gets measured is what gets done.

3. Balance your plate.
Women need to learn how to behave like a CEO, which is part of what I teach them. We need to do this in our ever-changing environments as well. We all wear different hats at different times but are still the same person with the same values. For example, we act differently in our place of worship, at dinner talking with our kids, talking business, and with our significant other or friendships. CEOs know how to adapt these behaviors, and that's why I say we need to bring out our CEO skills in order to appreciate life more.

When I am at home, my CEO hat is off, and I enjoy being a spouse and partner with the man I love so much. I also enjoy the friendships I have. Ultimately, if you believe you can manage it you will prove yourself to be true. What you think about is what you bring about.

For me, balance is achieved when I manage boundaries over managing time. I am clear on what I will not do, no matter how much or little time it would take. I only do what I want on my plate that makes me feel good.

4. In business, you need to always be reviewing the product or service you offer.

The people who know me well have heard me say how the scenery only changes for the lead dog. I want to look at the sky above and the air in front of me instead of copying someone else. Jeff Bezos says, "Everyone keeps their eye on us. We're keeping our eye on the customer."

In my life, not a day goes by when I don't talk about being the innovator—an early adapter in my space is what I want to be. What are other people doing that I can adapt and implement? It can be risky and not everyone believes in you right away. Take note: eye-rollers indicate that you are onto something.

5. Processes

You can't duplicate and replicate if you don't have processes in place. Consistency is the process that gets you there and persistence keeps you there.

6. Performance

Know what matters and don't get caught up into the minutia of things. By the fifth day of the month, I need people's data from the previous month. This is where I find opportunities to discover areas of concern and can interpret numbers to give me solid data to work with.

What's not in there is the risk. I have invested a lot of cash to create success. Branding, tech, metrics, growing our membership and retaining it takes a financial investment. It goes contrary to what a lot of people say right now. I have learned you cannot run a business and live in the safe zone.

PRINCIPLE #5:
THE HUDDLE

"I feel that a great coach is one that has a vision, sets a plan in place, has the right people in place to execute that plan and then accepts the responsibility if that plan is not carried out."

―――――――――――

MIKE SINGLETARY

What defines a team? Is it the coach or the players? While a team is greatly capable of tremendous accomplishment, the coach helps unite everyone and create the framework for the team's success. They're also someone who brings people together to achieve a common goal. Developing the qualities to push through toward success takes time and effort, but in the end, that is the chance for magic to happen either on the court or with your personal goals.

In creating the framework for the vision of a team's success, the tone is set for all that happens afterward. This framework is instrumental for orchestrating results and when done properly, a successful season follows. However, no team stays the same forever. Not all collegiate level players become a starter during their college careers any more than a non-productive sales representative gets unlimited time to start delivering what is expected. When members of a team do not perform, changes are made in the huddle that impact the entire team's course of action.

Who gets to be a starter on a sports team is constantly evolving, depending on their skills and performance in comparison to other teammates. As new talents come in and others transition out or move to their next career step, a team's dynamics are changed. Similarly, as one person gets promoted in business, opportunities for new talent emerge to fill a need.

Over the years, Hawley has learned that different types and styles of leadership are needed to navigate the continually shifting culture of a team.

DIFFERENT STYLES, SAME HOPE: HAWLEY

My athletic journey has been molded by the personalities of the coaches I have had. As a young softball player, my first memories of having a coach revolved around my dad. He taught me many things, although I did not always enjoy playing for him. He was demanding, hard, and critical. This is one of the reasons I chose volleyball over softball in college. Despite this, my dad's style of coaching did teach me several fundamentals about working hard, dedication, and discipline.

After my childhood softball career ended, my college student/athlete journey started at United States International University back in 1988. During my three years at USIU, I had two different head coaches and three different assistant coaches. Although we were a Division 1 program, we were independent and did not belong to a conference. This meant that week in and week out we played against some of the top teams in the nation, with little recognition or success. Then, in my junior season, USIU dropped their entire athletic department because of budget cuts. I transferred to Arkansas State University in my senior year, where I had a completely different experience with a coach who had been at the program for many years and had built a winning tradition.

Each coach had different expectations on conditioning, diet, drills, studying the game, and overall philosophies. Even the expectations for being a student, curfew, and outside season activities were opposing. These differences molded my coaching style and how I approach my business today. I want to highlight the differences between three of these coaches to illustrate how important it is to create players and teams that want to build a championship tradition.

My first college coach was the type of person who wanted people to like him. Strict boundaries and discipline did not exist, and being your friend was what he desired.

With flexibility and no strict guidelines in place, the players were responsible for taking many of the initiatives. It is my understanding that this coach—who I really appreciate because he is the one who gave me a scholarship—took over from a very domineering coach. It makes sense that many of the older players wanted to have a relaxed atmosphere for their remaining volleyball seasons. However, for me, this type of coaching did not help me develop into my best self.

Granted, for some athletes this coach worked perfectly well. He was like the fun parent after a divorce: the one who wanted to be a friend. Although his coaching style was not for me, I am eternally grateful to him for giving me the scholarship that let me play volleyball at the Division 1 level and to help my dream of playing college volleyball come true.

Then, after my freshman season, our athletic director wanted to take the program in a new direction, so I got a new coach. This coach's philosophy and approach was like a dictatorship. He had a strict regimen in place. This was the first time someone outside of my family placed me on a diet because my body fat was not under 15%. It seemed like no matter how hard I worked out I could not drop under 17% and it was very frustrating. I would run miles (which was detrimental to my vertical) just so I would not gain weight and my coach would not ridicule me.

Our practices were scheduled down to the minute. If things were not going according to plan, i.e., if we were not winning, the new plan became getting into the best shape of anyone, regardless of talent level. One time we were playing the number one team in the nation, Long Beach State. We took a game off them right before they came back and crushed us. Our team was excited to take a game off such a powerful team, but our coach was disappointed. His punishment: sets of 15 for sprints, bear crawls, piggyback rides, burpees, crossovers, push- ups, sit-ups, and any other conditioning tool he could use. We spent an hour after the match in the parking garage, and then, on the van ride home, we were instructed to not say a word and there would be no post-game meal for us. His mode of operation was laden with punishment for unrealistic expectations.

I endured two years with this coach before USIU dropped their athletic program. Although it was tough, I did learn some valuable lessons. One concept was the importance of relentless pursuit. If he did not feel I was giving my best effort he would say, "Hawley, we need to see a little relentless pursuit. No ball is ungetatable until maximum effort is exhausted." Of course, if he did not believe I was going after the ball at full throttle then he would announce to the team that we would begin running lines.

Another thing I learned is that we can often go further with encouragement from others than we will by pushing ourselves alone, my body and mind can do more than I think, and conditioning is just one way to break through mental blocks that hold me back from greatness. I can do anything for 30 minutes, 45 minutes, or even an hour without quitting or backing down. One time, he had us do this blocking drill non-stop. Usually, in this drill, a player would jump about 18 times, going to the right and to the left, 3 sets of three each way. On this day, Coach had us do this drill for at least 45 minutes. We must have jumped, at a minimum, 135 times.

This coach had passion, but he lacked the emotional maturity that a seasoned coach uses for success. I believed he was attempting to be the common enemy, something that would drive our team to victory. He did not build the foundation before he demanded we follow his leadership or, shall I say, dictatorship. However, I did learn much from his style that I use in my own coaching, such as not to cut corners. For example, when warming up, this was as simple as making sure we did not cut the corners of the court. This is a technique I use when I am coaching kids in volleyball or adults in business. I learned hard work and grit. I learned how to go after something full speed ahead and only stop after maximum effort had been expended.

The third coach I had entered my life when I transferred to Arkansas State. This man had a clear and precise plan, as well as a passion for excellence. He had a great relationship with his players but there were clearly defined boundaries. Despite never playing volleyball (the other two coaches were collegiate players), this coach had a way of enrolling his players into the dream. In fact, one of the main reasons I transferred to Arkansas State is because of his winning record and his Southern voice saying to me, "You girls (he was recruiting me and my best friend April Devine) ought to come on down here and win yourself a conference championship ring." He was a student of the game and taught me how to be the same. My ASU coach was great at putting the right person in the right position. This built confidence, which led to greater self-esteem.

This was a tough time in my life because my father had just passed away. I don't even recall all of the season. However, specific exchanges and games had a tremendous impact on me. Besides, I have my best friend to help me remember how our team received a standing ovation from a sold-out field house at the University of New Mexico. We finished the season with 41 wins and only 8 losses. We won that conference championship ring that he promised and, more importantly for me, I had a coach who believed in me and taught me how to believe in myself.

These three coaching styles each helped form the person I am today. I would have never thought I could take away so many positives from the first three years of my college career. The approachability of my first coach, his willingness to take a chance on me and give me a full ride, helped me fulfill my dream of playing Division I volleyball. My second coach's rigid structure of discipline helped me establish some continuity in the face of uncertainty. I always pursue my goals with the same relentless gusto he taught me. Finally, from my third coach, I learned the kind and gentle guidance of a true ally on the sideline. As I write, I realize that this is one thing that helped to shape the leader I am today.

Getting people to believe they can do it, whatever that IT may be, is one of the greatest gifts you can give another human being. Looking at someone and really seeing them, being completely present in the conversation, is what I learned from my coach at Arkansas State. These three taught me valuable insights into the type of coach I always strive to be, and how I can manage growth within different frameworks. Their legacies have helped me develop my approach to team and leadership.

Carey also offers great insights on this but from a different perspective.

A TEAM'S SUPPORT: CAREY

Early in my collegiate career, our entire team had the opportunity to go to a team-building course, which is an outdoor obstacle course with many different exercises. Climbing ropes is one such exercise. Other examples include the trust fall and crawling through a narrow pipe under a large hill of dirt. This latter example really tested me. I was claustrophobic and the pipe we were supposed to crawl through seemed extremely small. It was also raining, making a lot of mud and water on the bottom of the pipe. I clearly remember my racing heart, and the lump in my throat as I held back tears in tremendous dread. Going into that pipe would be one of the most difficult things I ever had to do.

I made several attempts to crawl through, because I did not want to let my teammates down. On the first try I was so scared I simply couldn't do it. The coach and some players encouraged me, but I still could not go in. The conflict was heavy on my heart. Letting my team down would hurt me, yet I was so scared that it was almost paralyzing.

When it came time for another try, I got part of the way in and then wound up backing out of the pipe. This was not any easier, as the pipe was over eight feet long. Once I was all the way in the pipe, there was still a long way to crawl forward. Then I heard, "You can quit if you want."

I was soaking wet from the rain and mud. The lump in my throat was even bigger now, but I knew I had not yet reached my breaking point. You can do it, I told myself. Please God, help me through this.

This became my mantra to keep me going. With tremendous strength and fortitude, I faced my vulnerability head-on. I was finally able to get down on my hands and knees, then on my stomach, to crawl through the pipe. I still recall how tough it was when I reached the middle of the pipe. I heard the voices of my teammates encouraging me, several of whom had already made it through okay, and I saw the light ahead. The physical and emotional exhaustion remains vivid.

It was all worth it! Not only had I faced my fear of small spaces, but I also had earned the respect of my teammates. They proved to me that I could count on them to help me through one of the hardest challenges of my life. I had demonstrated my willingness to push through beyond my previous limitations. What is more, I had sacrificed for the good of our team. Several of my teammates had difficulty with this challenge, and my example helped push them forward. Sometimes we must sacrifice something in ourselves for the good of the team, even when facing a challenge and wanting to run away from it. This also applies in our personal lives.

Back in 2017, my younger sister was diagnosed with breast cancer—barely two years after recovering from a stroke. She was scheduled for a double mastectomy after her treatments ended—the final step in hopefully preventing her from going out of remission. During this time, my mother was battling arthritis and congestive heart failure and had been in hospice for six months; her life was nearing its end.

My family had to work as a team and simultaneously tackle these issues. This was a scary and emotional time and decisions had to be made quickly. Who was going where? Ultimately, I went to be with my sister, whose procedure was complicated due to uncertainties from the earlier stroke. Meanwhile, my dad, brother, and other sister were with my mom.

Luckily, we were all blessed to receive good news for my sister. After the surgery, she asked me to go tell Mom she was okay, and that the surgery was a success. I drove 45 minutes north to give Mom the amazing news. It was exceedingly difficult to leave my sister, but she needed me to tell our mother. When I got there, Mom was unconscious, peaceful, and pain-free, but her breathing was very labored. I turned on some of her favorite music, rubbed her hand, and told her about the success of the surgery. Tears rolling down my cheeks, I drove back south, not wanting to leave my dear mother, but I left knowing that Mom was in good hands and surrounded by family.

That night, as my sister and I fell asleep—I slept in her room to make sure she rested and that the nurses and doctors took care of her—I shared the story of my peaceful visit with Mom. Then, shortly after midnight, our brother called. The nurse appeared in the doorway and asked if everything was okay, since everyone there also knew about our mom's situation. My brother called with the news that Mom had passed away peacefully and without pain. Afterward, the nurse, my sister, and I prayed by the bedside.

All my family members had done the best we could, even with the distance between us. This is one of my most personal examples of just how crucial teamwork is, whether in sports or real life.

TEAM BUILDING 101

There is an exceptional book called *The Five Dysfunctions of a Team* by Patrick Lencioni. It discloses five ways in which teams do not work as effectively as they could: 1) Absence of trust, 2) Fear of conflict, 3) Lack of commitment, 4) Avoidance of accountability, and 5) Inattention to results.

Effective coaching helps eliminate these risky behaviors and replace them with effective, winning habits through team building. Organizations that are in touch with their goals' big picture recognize the importance of individuals, as well as their collective efforts. This way of engaging within a team positions people for success. This is the case at the beginning of a sports season, in the daily activities of a business team, and in families.

A functioning team begins with trust. You need to trust that other members are doing their part so that you can be committed to doing yours. You cannot be in more than one place at a time, so you need your teammates to cover all others. Whether you need to do more practice drills, take additional phone calls, or whatever, you must be reliable in doing your own part.

When everybody is doing what they are supposed to, you can cohesively work together and continue to push toward your goal. That means that each member is working hard to make the collective goal attainable. In our business, for example, thousands of presentations and thousands of hours upon hours are devoted to becoming solid in your position on the team.

Going above and beyond is what takes you to greatness. Once you get to that level of being able to perform well, dysfunction diminishes and teams achieve more together. It's comparable to a tug-of-war, with determined individuals wanting to take the winning shot and bring out their inner Michael Jordan.

Incidentally, the *Last Dance* documentary about the Chicago Bulls discussed this very thing. Michael Jordan realized that greatness was not on his shoulders alone, but a responsibility of the entire team. This epiphany made him more attentive to the results and how to maximize them.

YOUR DECISIONS WITHIN A
TEAM COMMITMENT

A commitment is when you dedicate yourself to a decision, like a cause or activity. When you give your word, can people count on it? Do you follow through? Are you committed? This could be a coaching call every weekday morning at 6 A.M. for 90 days. It could be a life-long relationship, like a marriage or a friendship. That commitment could be a business partnership or starting a company or new position. As your children grow, how does your commitment to them change? Have you ever really looked at your life closely and decided what things or people you are committed to and what things you are not committed to?

Answering these questions is a role of leadership. A coach, captain, or a team leader has a responsibility to ask these questions of the team, players, or family members, and help guide sound decision-making. At times, you will make the choice to move forward without asking for input or feedback. However, when the choices you make affect the entire organization, team, or family, you will want input. Otherwise, those under your command may not accept the decisions you make for them.

These points can be effectively driven home through solid leadership. A volleyball player could be confident they could sacrifice their body for the winning shot but still not succeed. In business, a person could try a different strategy to close a nice deal but be shut down. There are no guarantees our risks will work. Still, we all can have a reasonable expectation that those who lead us have good insights into the specifics of a situation. They know what did not work and why, for whatever reason. These lessons also carry over into other areas of our lives.

FOUR RULES OF TEAM ENGAGEMENT

For a team to succeed, all its members need to be functioning at a high level. This is how to achieve accomplishments and earn successes. This is exemplified in four important ways, which become your rules of engagement.

1. Learn how to effectively manage conflict

People often avoid conflict when, in fact, they should take steps to address the conflict with those who are directly involved. You should first work to have a conversation while the disagreement is smaller, before it becomes a mountain. Catch yourself before you speak to others not involved and redirect the conversation to the person or people directly involved in the conflict. Do your best to listen to the other point of view and understand why they might feel the way they do. Listen to understand. Do your best to not listen to respond, attack, or be defensive.

If this step doesn't work, ask a third party to act as an objective mediator. This can be a coach, leader, manager, friend, teammate, or colleague: someone who may be able to focus the conversation on a common goal to resolve the dispute. Conflict can be difficult yet avoiding it or sweeping it under the rug can lead to larger, more difficult situations. That's why trust is so important. It builds an open environment to discuss different opinions and perspectives so all parties can agree on the best course of action. These are methods for healthy resolution to a problem, including serious issues.

2. Act and evaluate results

Decisions are made and actions are taken based on what is needed or desired. Then comes the test run where you give the idea time to be implemented, and then evaluate its progress. In Hawley's work, she is the head of the Technology Committee and sometimes ideas are presented to her that she must react to. She might learn more about a topic or idea, and then revisit it in a few months, or she might act on it and then evaluate that idea's results after a period. Only when you put something into practice can you see how it works.

All situations need to be evaluated differently based on their merit. When someone is on the right path, such an accomplishment is noted and questions are asked to learn how and why it worked. The same is true when the wrong path has been chosen. Breaking it down into parts is essential for learning and growth, regardless of whether it is in a relationship, product or service, or a pathway to success.

3. Recognize your role and contributions to the team

The relationships we make in life play a role in defining the level of happiness and success we have in our lives. This is true in business just as it is in our personal lives. Teammates are members of committees, boards of directors, work teams, family members, and athletic teams—individual contributors to a group effort. A team provides a structure in which people are valued, respected, and have an opportunity to contribute to the collective effort. This collaborative mindset leads to greater levels of success and fulfillment.

Each team member has their strengths and areas where improvement is needed. When each teammate works in their areas of strength, or highest and best use of their abilities, they will be more confident and their impact on the team success will be stronger most of the time. As more and more team members perform in their highest and best abilities, the more the team will thrive.

4. Developing leadership

Leadership is not stagnant. It is growing, changing, and flowing as opportunities and situations arise. Being able to know your starting point is important. Once a project is complete or close to completion, it is vital that a leader stays focused on the vision of where the team is heading. It is wise to be several steps ahead of the team. Developing a what's-next attitude will help you thrive. Additionally, as a leader, you always keep growing and keep surrounding yourself with people that will challenge you.

Another important part of leadership is the connections we make and how we relate to each person on the team. Understanding every member's "why" will help you identify each person's needs and how you can support and get the most out of the person's strengths.

Building strong leaders is an interesting dance of self-discovery for the person being trained and the one doing the training. It is easy to let someone off the hook for not stepping in or doing what they say they are going to do. However, no matter the circumstances, teams support each other, recognize when they need to intervene, and know when they need to take a step back to give everyone the elements to thrive.

THE DAILY PUSH

Take time to reflect on the following series of questions. Write your answers in your journal or use The Daily Push Journal.

1. Identify teams you are currently a member of and list them. Examples include athletic team, leadership team, board of directors, committee, non-profit, church group, family, etc.
2. What role do you play on each of the teams?
   a. What could you do to improve those teams?
3. What personal sacrifices have you made? Are you making these for the betterment of the entire group or organization?
4. Who are the leaders of each of the teams?
   a. What characteristics or traits do they possess that makes them a good leader?
   b. What actions have they taken to set the direction the team is taking or has taken?
5. What could you do to improve each of the teams?
   a. What improvements could the leader make?
6. What are you going to do to improve your role?
   a. What are you going to do to improve each team?

Reflection helps you identify where you stand in any situation, and in this case, your contributions to a team. It is imperative to understand what you could do to improve your role and the team. Once you understand this, it is time to make a commitment to whatever actions are required to help each team reach a higher level of success. When this flow is discovered it makes it easier to become "Fierce!"

AN INTERVIEW WITH DANELLE DELGADO

We were thrilled to interview the now serial entrepreneur Danelle Delgado. She began her journey while raising her three small children on her own. Forced to make a change she went from working three jobs at 80-90 hours a week and struggling to survive, to award-winning success in business. She accomplished this by aligning herself with some of the world's most renowned business experts and gained them as personal mentors. After years of high-level learning, she built some of the fastest-growing online business training companies to date. She is a renowned online millionaire maker and has made a massive impact from her international speaking career, her best-selling book *I Choose Joy*, and her unmatched skills guiding entrepreneurs both online and off. She is the owner of Life Intended, which delivers world-class training designed to equip driven individuals with tools to inspire action and attain results. Although her work is her heartbeat, she is blessed beyond measure with her three kids in Colorado and teaches them to live the life they are capable of.

What "push through" story in your life has contributed to your success?
I grew up an athlete and I have attacked everything I encounter in life with this same mindset. Gymnastics was my sport and it taught me to not feel pain until the job is done. An example of this happened one year during the state tournament. I was doing my routine on the balance beam and fell. Both my coach and I knew what happened right away—I had broken my tailbone. Then my coach gave me a look, letting me know I had better finish the routine, and so I did. Only after I got off the course and over to my coach did I let the tears of physical pain and disappointment roll down my cheeks.

This moment became a catalyst for everything I do. I still cry when it's over, never during. I've felt pain from divorce, cancer, and becoming an entrepreneur, but I've found a way to use it as a part of the process of acceleration, never to defeat me.

How has this fueled your success?
I have noticed that every time I have done well, a coach has helped me understand the steps. Everything I am today is a result of how I was raised and trained and coached.

Growing up, my family was always busy, which meant certain coaches became my mentors. They taught me that the general principles for success are the same across the board. Whenever you learn a skill, you begin with the basics, practice them to perfection, and then perform it. This is what I do both as a parent and in business. It has been my pattern throughout life. Learn – practice – execute.

In my work as a coach and strategist, when people start talking with me about the emotions and fears that hold them back, I tell them they are filling their brains with the wrong stuff. What a brain needs in life is growth, gratitude, goals, and principles. There is no room for emotional quitting. Put your principles in place and execute them every day. That way, you won't leave room in your mind for the things that make you weak.

What daily habits or routines do you have to pursue your goals?
Every day it is important for me to:

- Write down ten things I am grateful for. If a challenging day appears, I may write up to 100 things to keep my brain focused on good thoughts and actions.
- I devote 1 to 1.5 hours to growth learning every day. I really like audiobooks for what they offer.
- I have daily goals to achieve. I know what I am doing and have a plan in place to execute on it.

I never end my day at a net-zero. It is always a net positive, and there is no room in my life for the things that make people quit. To help with this, I have created a business bubble for myself, where I realize and control the input to control the output.

If you let external things come in and change your goal, dream, or target, it can hurt you. One step to controlling input is making sure you have the right coach for you. If you ever didn't get to pick your coach based on their qualities that would help you grow, you'll understand what I mean. I had this happen in gymnastics once. When I was on the bars and ready to release, I was a bit off, resulting in a crash and burn. It would have been easy to beat myself up for it, but I realized I wasn't in my own head as much as my coach was. This person had gotten under my skin and, unfortunately, I couldn't get him out that day, but it was the last day he had gained entry.

What are the most common things you have seen people let get in the way of their achievements?
Nothing stops a person more than fear. People use fear to not act, choosing instead, to think that what they desired was a mere dream. It's a result of output from different experiences and a lack of creating the practices to put into play. You start acting on emotions, not facts, and I believe people need facts over feelings every day.

It's all about what you lean into. I perform with positive reinforcement, good news, and the truth. I do not perform well under fear of loss and lack. You need to learn about what turns you on and what turns you off and then create the boundaries to control the input. For example, a salesperson operating under manipulation lacks skill and is not living in truth. This type of individual will not achieve better results until they start living in the truth. Once you tap into your own truth, there is no room to dwell on what others may say or assume about you. Not everyone needs to love you.

I would like to see people overcome this problem. Most do not have a big enough voice to drown out the lies…unless they have a mentor to help them in the process of finding the good truth.

What is the message you would give to readers to push through to their next level of success?
The number one thing I live by is adhering to principles that create practices. Practices, in turn, create results. The more we get to know ourselves and what we are capable of, the more we develop the principles that make our habits. I am a principled person who focuses on the basics and systems. I realize I didn't do this when I was not living by my own truth. Now, what doesn't fit gets removed. This is what I want to see happen for everyone: know who you are and what makes you win; you repeat it and get results. Win on repeat.

What about your legacy fires you up?
People make lots of money when they know their game. Training up people of value makes a difference in this world. Knowledge. Action. Impact. Knowing I have accelerated people's ability to earn so they can make an impact is awesome. It cements that if you could gather a group of humans and let them know their value, then nothing bad would happen—only good.

When it comes to women, how do you feel about assertiveness and aggressiveness in entrepreneurship?

Women were designed to be lionesses. We feed and hunt and care for and protect. It's in our nature and when we deny it, we deny who we are. Caring for people is not submissive; it's the greatest honor in the world. Aggressiveness with purpose will light women on fire. We were born to lead the pack and do that with love.

What can bridge the gap between your level of success and people on the rise?

Training is the number one bridge builder. Humans are one leap away. It takes an investment in the process and once this is done you cannot be the same person after. A paid investment to train takes you from normal speed to glorious acceleration.

PRINCIPLE #6: FIERCE!

"Courage, sacrifice, determination, commitment, toughness, heart, talent, guts. That's what little girls are made of; the heck with sugar and spice."

BETHANY HAMILTON

What does it take to be successful in a male-dominated industry? How have you been able to thrive and break through the "glass ceiling?" Why is equality in the workplace so important to you? What are you doing to help other women push through? We get these questions often. We assure you, without apology, that we did not make it to the top of our companies or industry by being meek, docile women. However, the criticism and critique are not completely accurate either. Crazy, mean, unapproachable, b*@#h, cold-hearted, unfriendly, aggressive, demanding, emotional, etc., are just a few of the name's successful women, including us, have heard during the climb to the top. It can be tricky to really know the balance of being assertive without being disrespectful, being competitive without being greedy, or being aggressive without being hostile.

Success requires the characteristics of being fierce, aggressive, assertive, and competitive. When women display these characteristics, it can be perceived differently in our ever-changing world. The pressure is often intense, and expectations of transparency are quickly established.

However, when a tough issue arises, you need to separate the emotions from the facts at hand. Again, this can challenge women because many were not raised to confront and control these moments.

If you want to be taken seriously, it often requires a certain amount of assertiveness on your behalf. The characteristic of aggression is an even more powerful tool to garner success if you can display it properly. This means having good intentions and not trampling others over. Today, women can be fierce and feminine, and as Coach Kiraly said, "beast mode" isn't offensive, it is an aspiration.

We all have certain beliefs around which we build our lives and business. When they clash with what we want to achieve, it's hard to figure out the proper strategy to put it all together and claim what it is you're working toward. Sports really helps in this area because it grants passage for people to grow past stereotypes. In fact, a global EY and ESPNW survey from March 2018 states that 94% of c-suite women have played competitive sports, and we both feel this has had a major impact on our professional accomplishments[1].

Many of those women may have learned to BE AGGRESSIVE the same way Hawley did when she played softball. There is a great cheer that was called out on the sidelines of some of Hawley's games that is applicable to those who want to reach the sky (and beyond) in business. It went:

"Be aggressive, B-E aggressive, B-E-A-G-G-R-E-S-S-I-V-E. Be aggressive!!"

Like a battle cry or an "I am" statement, these little cheers are usually taught to young female athletes to help them grasp what is expected of them in personal development and growth in the sport. We feel these same childhood cheers are powerful reminders that adults can take into the business world. You need to develop the ability to assert yourself confidently and be okay with being aggressive. Embrace it! Never apologize for your beast mode, because it is glorious when it's revealed on the court or when expanding your business.

For example, team members are often driven and inspired by incentives that require aggressive and competitive action to produce results. These qualities are meant to be a part of your career and we want everyone to achieve them, with or without prizes. No one can stop a proactive person who is driven and willing, pursuing their goals. It's powerful beyond measure, carrying over into all areas of life.

Let's hear Carey's take on this.

THE DEAL MAKER: CAREY

Until only a few years ago, I was honored to be the college recruiting coordinator for our volleyball club. It was a job that required hard work, a lot of time, and the ability to help the young club members be showcased to potential recruiters.

Important parts of my responsibilities were to:

1. Educate high school players and their families on how the recruiting process worked, what to expect, and how to communi-

cate with college coaches. Could they get placements to advance to the next level?

2. Proactively communicating with college volleyball coaches about what positions they are targeting based on specific graduation years.
3. Making appropriate connections between student-athletes and college coaches.
4. Guiding the recruiting process by arranging for the coaches to observe our student-athletes in practice and/or competition.
5. Assisting with the offer process and managing the rules associated with the recruiting process.

These responsibilities were also my goals. It was a difficult role, but I worked hard at it, and I was uniquely qualified with my experience on both sides of the recruiting process as a student-athlete and college coach. This role was a perfect opportunity to be aggressive, assertive, and competitive, all traits that are encouraged in athletics. I believed in what I was doing, and it was a fight worth taking because I am passionate about being proactive for the betterment of others.

Part of the energy I offered was a different strategy for making coach-to-athlete connections. College coaches are busier than you may realize, working 70-plus-hour weeks. Their time is valuable, and I knew this. I would proactively reach out to these coaches and make it as easy for them as possible during our communications.

Compare this to job searching. If you're trying to get a job, you must be ready for competition for whatever job position you want. No matter the position, there are a lot of talented people who want the same thing. You need to learn what makes you stand apart. I did everything within my control to make the girls in our club stand apart, so the coaches were able to watch them play, take their calls, and consider them for scholarship opportunities.

We took several steps to help our student-athletes stand out. These included proactive communication via email, text, and phone calls. We made sure the coaches knew our players' tournament and practice schedule. We followed up to make sure the coaches received our communication. I only communicated with them about players who met their priorities for specific graduation years. Also, the coaches relied on me to assist with matching up the level of ability to compete at their program's competition level.

I took the extra step of attending most major tournaments, including proactively approaching coaches by introducing myself and asking what they were focused on observing for the tournament. Often, I could bring them courtside for one or more of our student-athletes. This step made a huge impact and expanded the number of coaches observing our players. There was one tournament where the entire court was surrounded with college coaches from all over the country. Most of them were there because of the work our student-athletes and I had done both leading up to and at the tournament.

Over the years, this role gave me the opportunity to work with some of the most respected and best Division I and Division II coaches in the country. I even had about a dozen athletes receive full or partial athletic and academic scholarships.

Doing this work was a demonstration of persistence, competitiveness, aggressiveness, and assertiveness. I liken this to what recruiters do in the corporate world. They become a liaison for a qualified person and help place them in a position that fits their strengths.

Now, let's take a look at how Hawley learned about being competitive: something both she and I were attuned to by the young age of six.

ALWAYS BRING YOUR BEST GAME: HAWLEY

Every day, I see an opportunity to show the best of aggressiveness, competitiveness, and assertiveness. However, I do not always choose to be these qualities, there are days when it comes out naturally.

Throughout the years, I have been quite active with volleyball, either spectating, coaching, or playing. One time, my San Diego women's team was playing in a weekend tournament. That Friday evening, we went to a restaurant/bar with an outdoor volleyball court. We ladies were dressed up and set to have fun. We took our seats outdoors and immediately noticed this group of guys playing volleyball. They were dressed in rolled-up jeans and had their shirts off.

The guys were okay at the sport, but they were not free from our assessment of their performance. We watched with some amusement and then we heard one of the guys say, "Dude, you hit like a girl." This piqued the interest of several of my team members. One girl said, "Okay, who wants to play with me?" Another girl said she would. She was the ideal definition of a beast, a real power hitter who also happened to be a lefty.

There they were, ready to play. The rest of us ladies watched with a bit of excitement and curiosity. What would happen in this six-guys-against-two-gals match-up? The guys likely thought they had it in the bag; there was no way two girls could beat them. Early on, though, my teammates set the tone of the match. The power hitter went up to the ball and slammed it down. It hit this guy square in the head. Then she added, "That's how you hit like a girl." The guy who'd received the volleyball to the head turned fifty shades of red and it was hilarious.

To this day, we laugh about this story. It demonstrates, with a bit of humor, how a person can show a fierce, competitive nature with an attitude of sportsmanship and goodwill. And yes, when I go out with the volleyball women in my life, we still play, and people still like to see what we got. (We've still got it!)

Most of the best sports movies are the comeback stories. People love to see one, and it is a phenomenal example of what competitiveness, assertiveness, and aggressiveness can get you. More recently, I was in Hawaii watching a volleyball game, where my friend's daughter plays for the University of Hawaii. On this night, the Lady Wahines were playing their conference foe, the University of California at Santa Barbara. UCSB was ahead in the match 2 sets to 1.

The score was 18-17, in the 4th set with Santa Barbara leading the match. This is when Hawaii's setter erupted in intense competitive fire.

After a side-out (Hawaii got the ball back to serve) she headed back to the service line and started to rip jump serves, one ball after another, resulting in a 25-18 win for Hawaii. The battle was not over, though. Santa Barbara had a match point at 14-13, in the 5th set, but once again the Lady Wahines would not have it. The two teams took turns scoring: first 14-14, and then 15-15. Then, guess who headed to the service line...that's right! Hawaii's setter! In true comeback fashion, she blasted a match point for an ace, and the Lady Wahines won 17-15.

Let's break down what these young women learned and apply it to a business perspective. They learned time management, instantaneous decision-making, and communication, all of which are key to operating a business. They learned when to lead and when to follow. They learned how to be coachable, taking direction from peers and from their coach, perseverance in adversity, keeping emotions in check when the game is back and forth, etc. They learned teamwork and working together for a common goal. Finally, they learned their "beast mode," and how to take their performance to the next level.

In sports and business alike, there are times when a person decides to put the team on their back and just go for it. Their willingness to be aggressive and take the competition to the next level allows the entire team to be driven forward to victory. Seeing this play out in real time is awesome and inspiring. As both a coach and a volleyball fan, it is so fun to watch. It is equally amazing to watch people in business show how important their goals are and how they are willing to be fierce to achieve them.

Recently, I had a woman on my team who I had believed was going to quit and change to another career. However, she is still with the team and growing stronger daily. Since we've been working virtually more often, she has adapted to it very well. Her attitude is changed, and she has her entire team on board. Together, they are moving forward at an aggressive pace and it's impressive how she is embracing it! As she stated: "I just decided that I needed to change my attitude and show some competitiveness with myself and see how much I can do during this time."

Once you achieve something, you can never return to believing it's not possible. Few things are more powerful than a shift of mindset and attitude. The woman on my team exemplifies this and because of that, she is likely to qualify for some great incentives, which will continue to drive her toward new goals. These situations make for amazing comeback stories and are a driving force in achieving limitless results in business. These are people who have a voice to be heard.

YOUR VOICE MATTERS

In recent years, Hawley has been working to find ways to inspire women to be more competitive. Such a goal starts with being more assertive. Hawley has found that being an advocate for these women makes a big difference. We want to make strong and supportive women into strong and supportive teammates. However, regardless of whether you have a team of mostly women or a mix of men and women, the quality and individual character of all these people matter the most. Everyone wants to win in the end.

In sports, you may spike the ball hard to try and win a game. In golf, you may hit the perfect ball that gives you an edge. These are forms of aggressiveness and competitiveness. Compare this to the corporate world, where it aligns with the necessity to speak up for yourself and your ideas for improving performance and function within an organization.

We can all reflect on times when our voice was drowned out, stomped out, or simply disregarded. Some of us think, that's just the way it is, while others think, never again. We want you to be in the latter category. Never take a back seat and feel that your voice doesn't matter. Use this book and the journal to create the confidence you need to step up and out into your greatness. This is how you can achieve a W in the win column.

SOMEONE DOESN'T HAVE TO
LOSE FOR YOU TO WIN

Someone doesn't have to lose for you to win. If you understand this now, you'll be the better for it. Competition is often the fiercest when it is against ourselves. This is because we are the ones who eat, breath, and sleep our actions.

We are both incredibly competitive in our work. However, it is not against other people, but rather our own abilities to place clients in the best possible outcome for their goals. We refuse to be the byproducts of derogatory thinking and action. So, we set our hearts on "win, win, win," because there is room for anyone in our business who offers credibility and initiative.

In business, you may not always win, even when you have done all you could to claim success. You can play your best game and still be outmatched. The key is giving your best effort. There's no shame in walking away with your head held high about your efforts.

Competition pushes us beyond where we were previously limited. This is a glorious gift because it gives us insights into the ways in which we can push ourselves, work harder, study more, innovate, and find new methods to go beyond what we previously thought we could achieve.

As Hawley has said about her team: "Over the last few years, as our team has developed, we've all helped each other rise and do better than we have ever done." She also adds that while some teams they compete with have done better, that doesn't dissuade Hawley's team from doing better than they've done before. It's a constant assessment followed by strategic action.

Carey's firm hired a consultant recently and has done some joint work with people who are experts working with small business owners. This is the innovation, development, and drive they demonstrate to be competitive in their market. Their willingness to rise beyond where they once were will make a difference. The willingness to step outside of their comfort zone and beyond what they previously have accomplished helps drive them to break through to previously unseen levels. As Thomas Jefferson said, "If you want something you have never had, you must be willing to do something you have never done." This new frontier is achieved by gaining the qualities that move you forward.

3 FIERCE QUALITIES TO PURSUE

There are many qualities that define a fierce person. This is an individual who knows how to pursue their goals with the right levels of assertiveness, aggressiveness, and competitiveness. This is their "beast mode," and when you meet someone in this zone, you immediately recognize it through their style of leadership, their convictions in their beliefs, and a desire that ignites a flame.

Let's dive into each one.

1. What type of leader do you strive to be?

Most leaders are assertive, aggressive, and competitive. They didn't get to their level without these qualities and being unapologetic about it. You should celebrate these qualities because they are a guide for you to flourish in your own career. You need to still be aware that it's necessary to walk a fine line at times. Sometimes you overstep it and need to return to the attributes within these qualities that make you great. Rebound. Recover. Move forward.

2. Does your conviction carry you through to victory?

The things you believe in are worth fighting for. This means your perspective must be heard, in a meeting for example. There are times when being passive means losing out on an opportunity. This translates into the corporate world where decisions are made, and you need to speak up and fight for your idea or point of view. It takes a fighter attitude to recognize how much your voice matters, particularly when you have the conviction to follow through afterwards.

3. Is your desire strong enough to light your world on fire?

This is how you make your ideas and vision contagious. No matter what it is, you must be willing to fight for it, using all the grit you can. This is one of Carey's favorite aspects of being a coach, her willingness to put it all on the line.

Where do you stand with these three qualities that define a fierce person?

What do you still need to work on? You are a capable and magnificent person who can develop these skills to move forward into the successes you have only dreamed of at this point.

THE DAILY PUSH

We can manage our aggressive and competitive spirit in a healthy manner. We have all had times where we chose to be passive or occasionally been overly aggressive. Reflecting on the reasons behind this is important, which is why this is a part of this chapter's Daily Push.

We want you to reflect on various situations in your life, contemplating how they played out. If they did not work as hoped, how could the outcome have shifted? Take time to do each of these reflections; there is no need to rush.

Contemplate…

1. What was a situation where I did not control my aggression and it went too far?
    a. What happened as a result?
    b. What did I learn?
2. What happened when I stopped myself from speaking out in key situations?
    a. Do I reflect on them, thinking "What if?"
    b. Could I have made a positive difference if I had spoken up?
3. At what time in your life did you have the proper alignment of assertiveness, aggressiveness, and competitiveness?

a. How did you feel about this as it happened?

b. What made you realize you were in a sweet spot?

As you can tell, self-talk is an internal response with a significant impact. What we say to ourselves matters more than a word anyone else can say. Those who want the best results think about what they did, what they should be doing, and where they want to go.

For the second part of this exercise, we want you to write an account of your passive behaviors. Then, reflect on how you are going to change them so they become part of your healthy competitive spirit. The chart will help you to remember when you are passive and then state specific ways you can change. Be aware of what you put on the chart so you are attentive to moments when you can become brilliantly fierce in moving out of the passive zone. How could you be more assertive, aggressive, and competitive?

Here are some examples:
- Be proactive.
- Speak up for your ideas.
- Follow up even when you're unsure of the outcome.
- Ask for the assignment or opportunity.
- Stay longer and do the research for a project or come in early to make the extra effort.

Situation	Passive Behavior	New Proactive Response

You can be certain that the next time someone passes you over, or chooses to ignore your words and ideas, you have a healthy way to let them know, "I am here and I am ready to compete. Bring it on!" Turn up the dial to the more assertive you. Be the more aggressive you. Compete for what you want. When you do this, you are a step closer to "Triumph!"

AN INTERVIEW WITH MEHRAN ASSADI

Mehran Assadi is an inspirational leader, Chairman of the Board, CEO and President of National Life Group. His insights as a leader are a constant source of motivation. He was raised on the values of Do Good, Be Good, and Make Good. That commitment is at the heart of the mission-driven leadership principles ingrained in the culture of National Life. Their mission is to serve others. That is the compass that has guided Mehran's journey from entry-level software engineer to head coach.

We are honored to have him as an ally in the financial services industry and as a friend.

How did you develop your approach to leadership?
My dedication to servant leadership was inspired by two especially important people: my parents. You don't have to look far to find ideal role models, as they are often found at home. My mom and dad have always been the best role models.

My dad was a senior military leader. He always knew that it was a privilege to lead, not a right. He had a personal commitment to help others and put their needs ahead of his own. It was amazing to see how he treated those he worked with. Dad was firm, deliberate, and highly respectful. My mother is a natural-born leader. While raising the four of us, she also made time to advocate for women's rights, lead charitable activities within the community, and reach out to local youth. Our door was always open, and all were welcome.

You make servant leadership sound like a sacred commitment. Is it?
Servant leadership is critical to a successful culture. People have suggested that there is a religious element to my practice of servant leadership. I respectfully disagree. However, there is a spiritual element—that is, accountability to something that is bigger than you. It is woven into the personal commitment to those you work with and lead.

What daily routines do you follow to help guide you?
I am a creature of habit. I like to start my day at the gym, regardless of whether it is a day in the office or I am on the road. I get there by 5:30 a.m. and think about the day ahead as I exercise. I decide how I want my day to play out and what I would like to accomplish, my priorities, etc.

Daily connections with people are a priority. National Life is not a traditional company. We operate as a family. We are a differentiator who recognizes the importance of building strong relationships with distribution and our associates. If I'm not with my family, I am usually breaking bread with someone who is either a partner or teammate.

How do you live up to these standards you set for yourself?
Every Sunday morning for the last 25 years or so I have one highly structured weekly habit that I do. Before anyone else is up, I put on a pot of coffee and intentionally reflect on the previous week and the one to come. I use Norm Blake's 7 Cs of Leadership to manage this assessment.
- Comprehension
- Competency
- Confidence
- Courage

- Conviction
- Communication
- Character

This is my approach to personal accountability as a head coach.

Can you explain them a little bit more?

With the 7 Cs, Comprehension is about knowing what is around the corner and being ready to react to it. This is the primary role of a CEO and one that requires Competency, which is the foundation of knowledge you need to lead from. Once you have this you can generate Confidence in your knowledge, which gives you the ability to think ahead and be strategic. This allows for Conviction to surface, which means you are not wishy-washy in your approach to managing tasks. An example of this is when I joined National Life as a permanent employee. When I stated that we were going to do $100 million of life insurance and annuities a year, people could not see it. The company at that time was 150 years old and had never done that. I saw it differently; when teams learn how to win, they can finish and win even if they are down 20 points.

Communication is not tied to how well you write or speak English. It refers to communicating in a way that your audience can digest and appreciate what they are hearing, not using a bunch of fancy words.

With Character, you develop a level of trust and a sense of ethics—not playing situation ethics. It is about doing the right thing and being worthy of the trust placed in you.

The 7 Cs of leadership give me visibility to how I show up and how I am perceived & received by others. They are always at work as I go about my day.

PRINCIPLE #7:
TRIUMPH!

"Leadership is not about titles, positions or flowcharts. It is about one life influencing another."

———————————

JOHN C. MAXWELL

Have you ever had one of those moments where everything came together and finally made sense? This is one of those moments right now. You are at the place where you can see how all the dots connect. All that remains is for you to get to work on outlining your playbook and executing your game plan.

Whether you are an aspiring leader or looking to improve, you can now put together your playbook and begin to use it. Take it with you on the court or into your next business meeting or endeavor. Take it with you to your next committee meeting. Take it with you to your next family function. It will help you wherever you choose to go.

A great leader is this type of person: a proactive and assertive individual who also has humility and empathy and holds themselves and others accountable through tough love.

We all need these people in our lives! They inspire us to work together to create a winning plan that in turn creates a triumphant ending. Working together and holding each other accountable will also eliminate egocentricity and help produce the best possible outcome.

Of course, even the best leaders need help to push through obstacles and resistance. We sometimes need others to help us see what's on the other side of a roadblock. They offer the valuable nudge that you need and will ultimately appreciate.

Hawley has seen this firsthand in her journey with her company's CEO. She has been with him for many years and his growth is never stagnant. He began with fifty agents and now has thousands. This is a result of staying connected to growth strategies and ways to lead a team to better results. He had a bigger vision and needed to continually develop skills to ensure it came to fruition.

Similarly, take the epic documentary series *The Last Dance*, where we learn how Michael Jordan became a better, more complete player. At the beginning of his career, he saw himself as the one everyone counted on to win the game. As he matured as a player, he realized that he was not the only one who should take the buzzer-beating shot. In certain critical times during championship games, he passed the ball off to a teammate and they made the shot instead.

These examples show how leaders should offer directives that inspire us to perform better, whether on the court or in business. Today, top CEOs crave learning and knowledge that they can apply to their respective businesses. For example, they may go to a mastermind retreat to find new solutions and concepts to help them pioneer a stronger, more dynamic team into the future.

There are many ways to become the powerful force you've only envisioned thus far. Let's look at some insights Carey has learned over the years.

STEPPING STONES: CAREY

There are so many incredible inspirational leaders. Whether they are a CEO, team captain, manager, coach, etc., they make positive impacts in what they do. When you are willing, you can learn so much from them. I enjoy studying the journeys of these types of individuals and am grateful for how they help me grow. Here are several examples of powerful leaders in my life.

One of the first times I consciously realized I needed guidance and support was in a high school speech class. Like many, I was terrified to speak in front of others, and I longed to be rid of that fear. My teacher helped me gain the confidence to be able to deliver a speech in front of a group of peers and do it well.

Also, in high school, my basketball coach had a profound impact on me. Remember, he had elevated me to the varsity team after I had moved to a small town in mid-season—a bold move on his part. Even greater was his support for me and my love of volleyball, despite it not being the sport he coached. When I made it onto a volleyball team that traveled to Europe to compete, he did a truly kind and poignant thing. He started and organized a fundraiser so that I could afford to go. My coach wanted me to have the opportunity to experience something new and see how I could grow from it. I strive to emulate his unconditional support, as he did one of the most effective things a leader could do.

Then there was my club volleyball coach, who was also an assistant college volleyball coach at a university that had recruited me. She was a wonderful presence; from the way she coached the team to how she supported our ambitions. When I chose another college to attend, her response was fabulous. She humbly looked out for me, understanding what I needed to become my best. Then she helped me learn the position of setter, the role I would be taking on at Northwestern.

Being more prepared than I might have been otherwise meant a lot when I started my collegiate career. That infamous day where I got smashed in the face with a volleyball and my new coach's response to it helped me realize how fortunate I was for the opportunity. Make no mistake, without my opportunity to earn a full scholarship for volleyball, there was no way I could have afforded to attend Northwestern. There was no room to squander this opportunity of a lifetime, and once there, I found a great group of women and coaches that helped me get past all obstacles. It was an experience I likely would not have received anywhere but Northwestern.

I've taken all these lessons from my leaders and applied them at different times in my life, including during my career today. When I started working in the financial services industry, there were so many men and women who gladly shared their best practices with me. I attended conferences where industry leaders explained how they earned success and built their businesses. Even now, I never miss these conferences because I continue to learn so much about personal accountability in leadership from them.

The final advice is that there is an ebb and flow in knowing when to step up and be assertive or take a step back and let others take the initiative. When should I be ultra-competitive, like I was in the Big 10, or when should I dial that back for the good of our team? Realizing this is both fulfilling and rewarding when it is put into practice.

Now, let's discover how Hawley has experienced triumph.

MY UPWARD TRAJECTORY: HAWLEY

My first job as a teenager was at Jack Murphy Stadium where the San Diego Padres and Chargers played. I started off as a hotdog maker in the Sports Club and made my way up to manager in the Roof Garden just before turning 18. Then finally, I turned 21 and became a Skybox attendant. The suite I worked in most often was, oddly enough, the owner suite, where the owners of the Padres and the Chargers watched the game. Each of them was quite generous and I had the opportunity to meet a lot of influential and high-level people.

After working in the Padres' owner's box for one season, I was placed next door to serve one of the software companies affiliated with the owner. During that year, I made some great relationships, contacts, and even ran into a former teammate who worked for the company. Many times, the CEO and VPs would attend games with their families. During one visit, I struck up a conversation with the wife of a VP of International Sales. As we talked, she asked me about my background, and I shared that I had a degree in International Business. That night when they were getting ready to leave after the game, this woman said to her husband that he ought to hire me because I was more than qualified. We all laughed and then went our separate ways.

The next time that VP came in, he said to me, "Are you ready? Today's your interview."

He then introduced me to his team: the company's international sales leaders from across Europe, South America, and Asia. It was an eclectic group of leaders in high positions. If the game ended and they were raving about me, then I would have a job with the company. Luckily, when you give me a challenge, I tend to rise to the occasion, so this was going to be exciting.

A great idea came to me in an instant. One of the famous specialty foods at Jack Murphy Stadium was Rubio's Fish Tacos. If I could introduce the team to this unique food, and they all at least tasted them, then this would be a good test of my persuasion skills; it would also show initiative.

Although this food was a novelty, I was able to encourage everyone to try the tacos and they loved them; some of them even wanted more.

When the game ended, the VP of International Sales invited me to the office for a formal interview. At that point, it was just a formality as he let me know he wanted me to come on board!

I spent four years at the software company, where my boss received eight promotions. Every time he grew and developed, I moved along with him. I started as an administrative assistant, then a sales assistant, then an executive sales assistant, then executive worldwide sales analyst, until finally, I went into telesales. It was an incredibly rewarding chance to study under a dynamic leader.

Watching my boss engage with people, I learned that you always communicate with respect, whether it's with the janitor or CEO. He never failed to treat people well, even in his elevated position, which I'd watched evolve from VP of International Sales all the way to Chief Operations Officer. He was, simply put, one of the best leaders I had the privilege of learning from.

On the other hand, there are also situations that require self-leadership. You need to know where you are going and which of your strengths will take you the distance. I sometimes get triggered by the wrong motivation. If something pulls my attention, I struggle against it until I learn to work through it. An example of this is the process my husband and I underwent to get guardianship of our nephew.

Faith is a component of a business that we rarely hear about, but it was evident that divine intervention occurred in how our nephew came to live with us. Our story began with our nephew Adrian spending the night after a family barbeque. In the middle of the night, we got a call that Adrian's mom had been arrested. Once we found out that she would be serving a couple of years on drug charges, we went to work obtaining legal custody. We needed this so we could enroll him in a new school, get him medical coverage, take him to the dentist, sign him up for sports, and any other activity that requires a parent's signature.

Then we found out we needed more documentation than the extensive amount we'd already provided. The biggest challenge we faced was contacting his biological father, who had never had any contact with our nephew.

Researching this man's name and possible age was all we had. I started to call through the phone book and could not find anyone. In our first court appearance, we presented to the judge and he didn't think I had tried hard enough to locate Adrian's father. Therefore, he wasn't going to give us even temporary guardianship. Then, somewhere inside of me, a switch flipped and I told the judge, "We cannot enroll him in school, make sure that he has health insurance, take him to the dentist, even sign him up for sports without the guardianship. As we found out, this child had been neglected for eleven years in some basic areas of life, and we want to make sure that never happens again. Not while he is living with us."

I went into a mode of advocacy that we needed to make this happen. This was a moment where I had to fight like he was my own child because his best interest was at stake. Thankfully, our persistence paid off because we got temporary guardianship that day. We were more prepared for our next court appearance, four months later. I could tell the judge the number of people in jail in California, as well as in the rest of the nation, who shared the same name—324. I had contacted everybody in San Diego with the last name of Rodriguez and fitting the vague description.

Finally, my husband and I believed we found Adrian's father, who was living only a couple of blocks away in a jail in Southern California. My husband had an appointment to see this guy in person so he could confirm whether he had fathered Adrian. On the drive to the jail, my husband decided against the visit. He decided this man was not a suitable person for our family to have any connection with. Then later, when we went in front of the judge and told him the work we had done, the guardianship was finally approved. Despite the difficulty and frustrations we experienced, I believe the guardianship program is set up to make sure that you are fighting for the child, just like most people would do for their own children.

Life is filled with situations where you need to stand strong and fight. It is also filled with moments when you need to place your full trust in God and know He is going to protect and help you. Several months before, when Adrian's mother was in denial of her drug addiction and criminal associations, all we could do was pray that Adrian's safety and best interest would be taken care of. When Adrian's mom finally got arrested, it was like a greater plan unfolded for Adrian to get a chance for a different life. Now a grown man, Adrian serves our country in the Navy. He would likely never have had that opportunity had we not intervened for his own good. In leadership, as in all areas of life, empowering others is a selfless and good move.

THE EMPOWERING LEADER

To empower another person means surrendering your own ego. As leaders, we try to identify when that's not happening and when someone (maybe even us) is being self-centered or self-absorbed. These are poor attributes for any team member to have hardwired into them. However, it is possible to get back on track. Take corrective action by identifying when it happens, redirecting the person to get back in alignment, teaching them a better way, and empowering them to take the lead of something based on their strengths

A good leader doesn't take the reins in every situation: they encourage their teams to be confident enough to pave new roads of their own. That can inspire a great sense of triumph. Usually, the best compliment a person can receive is having built up a position that will eventually require a successor. That is, they have taken their job seriously, and their dedication has left a better legacy. That way, their successor will have fresh energy and ideas to take everyone another step further. With an encouraging and respectful team structure in place, this process keeps repeating itself.

Every organization needs a structure that empowers its members to keep on improving. If they don't, then it is not an organization that encourages growth. Always place yourself in a position where you can develop leadership skills as part of your plan of succession. When people empower each other, incredible results reveal themselves. We must always be ready to sacrifice the "me" for the "we" of the team. This is how leaders are developed.

BUILDING A GREAT LEADER

As the formula for a great leader has developed throughout this book, many defining moments have surfaced. Some leaders stand alone as much as they help aspiring professionals stand apart. When combined, however, they lean toward triumph and the satisfaction that stems from individual growth in a team environment. When doing this, their attributes help to cultivate and build a great leader.

1. Integrity

Although we mentioned the importance of integrity earlier in the book, we must remember that this trait is one of the single most important components to success. If you are trustworthy and have the reputation of being dependable, you will be given more opportunities for leadership. You will be selected to be on committees and teams that will help you become the leader you want to be. People who do not keep their word are often overlooked for promotions or chances to prove themselves.

You must demonstrate your values through your actions. You have probably heard, "walk the walk, not just talk the talk." We cannot stress enough how important this action is. When faced with difficult situations, where the difference between right and wrong seems blurred, take time to reflect, ask for input from people you respect, and make your best decision accordingly. The best leaders are relied upon to take the high road, even when it is the unexpected or less-traveled road. Do your best to help others reach those conclusions as well. Use those difficult situations as learning moments for those you coach.

2. Self-care

Taking time for yourself is essential to being a leader. You must know what activities/people fill your emotional and physical tanks and which deplete them. Most leaders do not learn this early on and thus experience burnout. If you have heard of the work-hard-play-hard philosophy, you may be familiar with the luxuries people take when they are successful. This isn't necessarily for show. It can also be a way for high performers to unplug from the stresses that come with being constantly on full alert.

This can be especially challenging for leaders who wear multiple hats in the workplace and at home. When you must be constantly available for a work situation (24/7 in some cases), your ability to relax becomes more difficult. One solution is to set boundaries. This is especially important when you work with your spouse, since keeping business at the office and the family at home can get blurry. However, the rewards outweigh the challenges.

Another recommendation is to figure out what activities help you relax or give you energy. This could be working out, playing a sport, getting a massage, reading, napping, going to the beach, taking a vacation, etc.

Discovering just how much rest you need is also important. For some, a 2-week vacation sounds like a dream come true, where others might find 7 or 10 days to be their sweet spot. Regardless, it is important to recognize that down time is needed to perform at an optimal level for a longer duration.

3. Emotional Intelligence

Emotional maturity is being able to step away from and manage your emotions. It is the ability to be objective about your emotions, so that you can reflect upon and understand how you react emotionally to certain situations. In the book *Emotional Intelligence 2.0*, authors Travis Bradberry and Jean Greaves reflect on four areas that, when developed, will help you maturely face difficult, demanding, or tense situations both in life and in business. Self-Awareness, Self-Management, Social Awareness and

Relationship Management are their areas of research and training toward personal competence.

The authors further explain that Self-Awareness refers to a person's ability to recognize an emotion. That is, we gain mastery when learning to observe an emotion rather than simply reacting to it. Secondly, Self-Management relates to your ability to act or to not act by assessing your emotions to make the most appropriate choice for the situation. Mastery comes when you can actively choose what you say, do and how you act at any moment.

Bradberry and Greaves then discuss Social Awareness. This component includes getting a sense of how people are feeling by being an active listener, as well as watching other people. "Social Awareness is about looking outward to learn about and appreciate others."

Finally, they examine Relationship Management. With this component, the authors illuminate your ability to use your awareness of your own emotions and the awareness of others. This helps to ensure clear communication, as well as foster greater mutual understanding and better managing of conflict when it arises.

4. Mindset matters

In Carol Dweck's bestselling book *Mindset*, she describes the difference between a fixed mindset and a growth mindset. A fixed mindset comes from the belief that your qualities are carved in stone, that characteristics such as intelligence, personality, and creativity are fixed traits, rather than something that can be developed.

A growth mindset comes from the belief that your basic qualities are things you can cultivate through effort. Yes, people differ greatly in aptitude, talents, interests, or temperaments. However, everyone can change and grow through application and experience. If you have made it this far in our book, you are most likely working to develop your growth mindset.

5. Passion, Fun, and Sense of Humor

It is rare to find a leader who cannot have fun and laugh at themselves. This is one key to staying sane on the rollercoaster that can come with leadership. There will be times when your ideas fall flat, when you make a mistake, or when you fail miserably. Despite these mishaps, you must stay passionate about your end goal. You must also stay connected to your vision. Not taking yourself too seriously will serve you well as you ascend.

Expectations are tricky, as Karch Kiraly mentioned in our interview with him. If you can manage your expectations and not get too high or too low emotionally, you will be much happier through the process. Passion, fun, and laughter does not mean that it will not be hard. Anything worth having comes with hard work. On the court and in business, it is essential to have a great work ethic, but the passion that drives you can be fun and lighthearted.

THE DAILY PUSH

Take time to reflect on the leaders in your life, whether in athletics, at work, your religious organization, your family, etc.

1. What did you learn from them?
2. How do you emulate them?
3. How have you demonstrated those same skills in your life?
4. What areas need development or improvement?

It's time to put all your different Daily Pushes into one exercise. We want to wrap it up tightly to create the ultimate playbook for your life.

Let's begin by doing this inventory of how you think you rank in each of the principles we have covered in this book. You will rate yourself on a scale of 1-10, with 1 being "needs a lot of work" and 10 being "I've got this."

Push Through Assessment:

Practice, Practice, Practice – Discipline, Routine, Time Management
    1   2   3   4   5   6   7   8   9   10

Just Keep Going – Perseverance, Resilience, Persistence
    1   2   3   4   5   6   7   8   9   10

Rise Up – Confidence, Courage, Humility
    1   2   3   4   5   6   7   8   9   10

Keep Score – Game Plan, Accountability, Decisiveness, Adaptability
    1   2   3   4   5   6   7   8   9   10

The Huddle – Being and Building a Team, Teamwork, Achieve Success
    1   2   3   4   5   6   7   8   9   10

Fierce! – Assertive, Aggressive, Competitiveness
    1   2   3   4   5   6   7   8   9   10

Triumph – Leadership, Self-Reliance, Execution
    1   2   3   4   5   6   7   8   9   10

Add up your total score. 7 is your lowest score and 70 is the highest. What is your total score?

Based on what your score is, you will fall into one of these three categories:

1. Champion
2. Competitor
3. Contender

Here's the breakdown of each one:

Champion: 55 points up to 70 points
This is exciting news! You have a firm grasp on the best aspects of Pushing Through. The combination of qualities you show have made a difference in what you have accomplished and in the way you help your team secure victories. Your next steps would be to keep building new skills and challenge yourself to grow, and work to help others develop into Champions. Even if you are an 8 in one area on the assessment, switching it up to a 9 will help you become better in your current role and any new opportunities you receive.

Competitor: 30 points up to 54 points
It's inspiring to see how far you've come and exciting to help you get to where you want to be in your career. The strengths you have are assets you can carry the whole distance. What you need to work on will require some commitment on your part. We recommend that you give serious dedication to the Daily Push for these chapters, consider taking on a coach or mentor to teach you where you need improvement, and to use your journal to document your process, thoughts, and the visions of your rising success.

Contender: 29 points or below
You may feel disheartened by this, but we see it differently. We think you should be encouraged. At this point, you are an open slate who has only begun to explore your greatest potential. With coaching and being proactive in your own growth and development you can move up the ladder to become a Competitor and eventually a Champion. We believe in you. Now it's time for you to start believing in yourself.

GOING THE DISTANCE!

"Be the hero of your own story. Show the world the quality of your character, the strength of your resolve, and the size of your heart by finishing strong."

GARY RYAN BLAIR

Can you feel the excitement of this journey? We sure can. Through this book, you have learned a great deal about what it takes to become a champion. Whether on the court or in the business arena, your confidence is being built up as you create, study, and master your playbook for success. You know what you need to do, so now it's time to do it! You are prepared to:

- Focus on the Daily Push exercises
  Do the assessments
  Take the reflections seriously
- Create your goals and break them down into manageable parts
  Make a commitment to yourself to become more proactive in your growth
- Fully understand and embolden yourself through your mission, vision, and values
- Allow yourself to be inspired by great interviews with people who have achieved levels of success you are aspiring to
  Take note: everyone we interviewed attributed this part of their success to their daily routine and habits
- Find your accountability partner(s)—those who connect with your values, goals, and aspirations, and want to help you succeed
- Pass whatever professional or personal tests that force you to prove your commitment to your growth process
- With these steps, the seven principles we shared will move from thought to implementation in your life. It will be incredible! Each principle carries a valuable lesson.
- Practice, Practice, Practice!
  Through discipline, a routine, and time management, you understand how drive and hard work are required of you. Mastering the fundamentals takes practice, and you want to do what it takes. Without this, you cannot reach the next level because it is the foundation of all your successes.

- Just Keep Going

  You will be tested in life, which means you need perseverance and resilience. Then, when you inevitably reach a roadblock, you can tap into your developing habits. These will keep you focused on your progression and get yourself back on track.

- Rise Up

  With confidence, courage, and humility, you can move past setbacks. When one happens, you recognize that your only choice is to pick yourself up and continue. This is the perfect time to grow, learn, and take new strides forward.

- Keeping Score

  With a game plan in place, you can latch on to accountability, decisive action, and adaptability to best measure your results. You know the rules and parameters, and now you can check in and see how you're doing. It's your report card to see where your progress is leading you.

- The Huddle

  For your success, there is great power in building a team and being a part of one. This is what helps most people push through to the next level. It may require you to rely on others more than before or give up some of the "me" for "we." In the end, teamwork brings the drive that helps everyone rise higher than they would have on their own.

- Fierce

  Being assertive, aggressive, and competitive are admirable traits to have. Your "beast mode" is meant to be celebrated. When you learn to stand in your own power, unapologetic, you become comfortable leading or following to gain results for the greater good, no matter the situation.

- Triumph!

  Leaders are built up every day, showing people how to properly execute plans and master self-reliance. By this point in your journey, you have done all the work, invested in yourself fully, and are starting to see the results you aspired to achieve. Maybe some achievements are even beyond what you had hoped for.

These principles are all part of how you create a sound strategy for excellence through developing your playbook. They are the missing pieces you need. When they all start clicking, you will find a passionate and empowering energy you can use in every area of your life.

Heart matters so much on this journey. Let's hear what Hawley has to share about heart with you.

A HEARTFELT MESSAGE FROM HAWLEY

Think about the journey you've taken through this experience. It's about more than pushing through to a conclusion or viewing leadership as your only final destination. The magic is within the journey itself. It is true that whatever reward you gained from this journey feels sweet, but the real change—the profound change that got you the sweet reward—happens during the journey.

There is a quote by Marianne Williamson that encompasses my hopes for you:

> "Our deepest fear is not that we are inadequate. Our deepest fear is that we are powerful beyond measure. It is our light, not our darkness that most frightens us. We ask ourselves, 'Who am I to be brilliant, gorgeous, talented, fabulous?' Actually, who are you not to be? You are a child of God. Your playing small does not serve the world. There is nothing enlightened about shrinking so that other people won't feel insecure around you. We are all meant to shine, as children do. We were born to manifest the glory of God that is within us. It's not just in some of us; it's in everyone. And as we let our own light shine, we unconsciously give other people permission to do the same. As we are liberated from our own fear, our presence automatically liberates others."

Never shrink yourself to avoid others feeling insecure around you. We cannot control another person's insecurity. Therefore, we shouldn't alter our brilliant potential for anyone else's sake.

Experience has taught me that when I have not stood my ground, or been the person I needed to be, it was because I shrunk myself in the hopes that someone else would not feel insecure. It never worked because wilting doesn't help. However, if you stand and grow toward the sun, you'll have the power to experience and accomplish amazing things. These have been possible for me because of the lessons I learned through sports, and how they helped me grow stronger and more successful in the business world.

The glory of God is in us all and the principles we have shared here are meant to help you find your voice, and your rightful place at the table. Don't miss out on the abundant blessings life has to offer. Take the journey because it feels right so that you can manifest and reveal your potential to the waiting world.

All this is so exciting for me and for Carey.

A HEARTFELT MESSAGE FROM CAREY

This electrifying momentum is being created as we speak. Do you feel it igniting within you? Have you caught yourself saying "push through?" Have you encouraged someone else to practice one or more of the strategies within these pages? People are attracted to the principles shared in this book for a reason. As we said in our opening chapter: "What are you going to do about it?" So many people take a class, read a book, or attend a workshop, but never use or implement what they learned. Make this time different!

It's time to see how these strategies play out in your life. You owe it to yourself to try and see what a glorious difference your results could make, and, if necessary, try and try again. Through the stories shared in this book, we have also shared ways to win. Some of our ideas may work for you, or you may need your own ideas, but either way, we are here to assist you.

To accomplish this, you need to set goals and continue to assess your actions along the way. Use the reflection exercises to identify your top priorities for change. As Danelle Delgado put it in our interview, "Control the input." Give yourself the best self-talk, because the conversations you have with yourself will determine your course and be the signature on your actions. Pray, listen to your "Push Through" playlist, meditate, write in your journal, whatever tools work best for you. Those tools may be the strategies we have explored throughout the previous chapters, or that have worked for those we interviewed. Hold yourself accountable and remember you are not alone on your journey or struggles.

It is both an honor and an obligation for someone to be your accountability partner. Rely on these people to keep you on task for all you have said you will do. Establish a community where people can bounce ideas off each other. Hawley and I would be honored to be a part of that community, offering you inspiration and wisdom when required. The entire journey should bring out that which is good, positive, and happy in your life.

Let's all gain strength through becoming a community committed to executing our playbooks' plans and seeing where it takes us. Then we can reach out and guide others to their "push through" moments.

THE DAILY PUSH

You have completed each of the Daily Push exercises and completed the Push Through assessment. You have the foundational information you need to create your playbook. So, what are you going to do about it now? Will you continue down the path based on your old habits, or will you work to forge new ones?

You've read several stories throughout this book of specific strategies for shifting our mindset, routine, actions, and methods to push through. Now it's your turn to take some of these examples or come up with your own. What will you do daily? Weekly? What are your big picture goals and the incremental steps you will take to put yourself in the best position possible for achievement? Who will be your accountability partner(s)? Through our interviews for this book, we learned that every one of these people is committed to their daily routine. Many were also committed to a weekly routine, which is a part of this next exercise. To promote your growth, a thoughtful and thorough reflection is required.

They say it takes 66 days to change a habit. So, for this amount of time, you need to continually practice what it takes to ingrain an action or behavior into your subconscious until it becomes natural. There is no taking a day off and you are still on track. (Note: when you do this next exercise, if you take days off, you will have to start over. We really do mean 66 days! We encourage your accountability partner or partners to hold you accountable...)

Step 1: Complete one page per day in your My Daily Push Journal.

Step 2: We also want you to commit to 100% participation in this reflection once a week. The guidelines to give you the best success are:
1. Find a quiet place that is technology and people-free (aside from music that may lend to focus)
2. Do not rush yourself
3. Find takeaways from each area of evaluation (what you learned, what you need to improve on, what is working, etc.)

Everyone has a way to give this amount of time to their success every week. Here are the topics you will reflect on.

1. Practice, Practice, Practice
   a. What areas in the last week have you shown discipline, outlined a routine, or demonstrated strong time management?
   b. What areas in the last week need improvement or more practice in the week ahead?

2. Just Keep Going
    a. In the last week, how have you demonstrated perseverance or resilience?
    b. What can you do in the week ahead to improve and/or help others improve in their perseverance or resilience?
3. Rise Up
    a. This week, how have you shown confidence, courage, and/or humility?
    b. What can you do in the week ahead to work on and improve in these areas?
4. Keeping Score
    a. This week, what have you done to hold yourself or others accountable?
    b. What are some areas in the coming week where you can do a better job of keeping score?
    c. Have you checked in with your accountability partner(s) lately?
5. Huddle
    a. This week, what have you done to build your team or improve teamwork personally and/or professionally?
    b. How can you improve on or strengthen the teams you are a part of in the coming week?
6. Fierce
    a. Over the past week, when have you demonstrated assertiveness, aggressiveness, or competitiveness?
    b. Next week, what can you do to use these qualities to your advantage?
7. Triumph
    a. How have you demonstrated leadership qualities this week?
    b. What can you do to improve or enhance your leadership skills in the coming week and better execute your game plan?

Using concepts that you learned from reading each principle, evaluate your progress within these areas. Incorporate visualizations to support what you want to see yourself doing and how it feels to have accomplished them.

You are deserving of your triumph! Now it's time to start working to create it.

OUR DAILY PUSH CHALLENGE: LET'S CONNECT

We want to hear from you! We want to learn about your "Push Through" stories. The community we are growing is committed to:

- Idea sharing
- Prosperity
- Helping through challenges
- Camaraderie
- Being accountability partners

We all need a playbook to help us learn what it takes to push through life's situations and land on the podium, feeling victorious! Therefore, your participation in these pivotal topics is welcomed as much as necessary. Your involvement is what makes our entire community grow stronger together. We can thrive! So, let's connect:

1. www.pushthroughbook.com
2. www.thepushthroughmovement.com
3. Facebook
4. Instagram
5. LinkedIn
6. Twitter
7. YouTube

Thank you!

TESTIMONIALS

Push Through is designed for anyone who wants to live inspired and empowered daily. Woods and Yukich have years of coaching experience and have led individuals and teams to reach their full potential. They do a phenomenal job in applying the same principles from their sports playbook into a playbook for financial and life success. If you strive to achieve greatness and perform at a high level read this book.

ENDYIA KINNEY-STERNS, AWARD WINNING TELEVISION/FILM NETWORK EXECUTIVE PRODUCER

* * *

The ultimate playbook for people committed to success lies here. *Push Through* gives the reader a full plan on how to bring out the best competitor within them using valuable lessons learned in sports. When you apply sports strategy to personal and professional success, the results will surpass any expectations you set for yourself.

TODD STOTTLEMYRE, BEST-SELLING AUTHOR AND 3-TIME MAJOR LEAGUE BASEBALL WORLD CHAMPION.

We all need a play book to guide us, this book is phenomenal, read it over and over and implement the teachings & lessons to your daily life.

BOB PROCTOR, WORLD-RENOWNED SPEAKER, MOTIVATIONAL SPEAKER & BEST-SELLING AUTHOR

* * *

Push Through is a must-read for those of us who want to excel at this thing called life. The 7 principles Hawley and Carey share through their experiences as top-level athletes are spot-on and are lessons that easily translate to enjoying success in our day-to-day lives and careers. *Push Through* can help you achieve at the highest of levels. As I said, it's a must read!

DAWN E. WOLFGRAM, CLF®, WIFS 2020 NATIONAL PRESIDENT

* * *

Tired of spinning your wheels? Need a boost to your game plan for life and business? If you do, *Push Through* is the book for you. The authors' experiences as NCAA student-athletes and successful women business leaders provides a unique perspective in developing sound strategies in helping people reach their full potential.

BETH LAUNIERE - WOMEN'S HEAD VOLLEYBALL COACH UNIVERSITY OF UTAH AND AUTHOR OF STOP COMPETING AND START WINNING: THE BUSINESS OF COACHING

"I've personally had the honor of watching Hawley grow her business and brand and couldn't be prouder. To go a step further - she's looking back, identifying what worked well for her and sharing it to uplift and fast track others to success. A true leader is a giver at heart and that's what Hawley is."

TERRY KENNEDY - CHIEF EXECUTIVE OFFICER - APPRECIATION FINANCIAL

REFERENCE

[1] "Why Female Athletes Make Winning Entrepreneurs." ESPNW, 2017, assets.ey.com/content/dam/ey-sites/ey-com/en_gl/topics/entrepreneurship/ ey-why-female-athletes-make-winning-entrepreneurs.pdf.

RECOMMENDED RESOURCES

TrueWealth
Advising Group
Guidance Throughout Your Journey

WHAT DO WE MEAN BY
"Guidance Throughout Your Journey?"

- We collaborate with your professional advisors.

- We coach you when making and implementing important financial decisions.

- We integrate all aspects of your financial plan.

- We proactively communicate, update and clarify the complex.

- *We will work with and for you to achieve financial peace of mind.*

Contact Us Today To Schedule Your **COMPLIMENTARY, CONFIDENTIAL FINANCIAL ANALYSIS.**

Call Us At 219-779-9183

Business has never
been better

Retirement planning has skyrocketed at
Appreciation Financial.
We need YOU to help serve the abundance of
appointments that are set each day.

You Are:

*Coachable

*Motivated

*Accountable

*Hardworking

Have a desire to help
and serve others

MANTRAS WE LIVE BY:

✓ We help a lot of
people

✓ We create life
changing wealth

✓ We get better
every day

af appreciation
INSURANCE & FINANCIAL SERVICE